# MIND OVER MEMES

# MIND OVER MEMES

## *Passive Listening, Toxic Talk, and Other Modern Language Follies*

## Diana Senechal

ROWMAN & LITTLEFIELD
Lanham • Boulder • New York • London

Published by Rowman & Littlefield
An imprint of The Rowman & Littlefield Publishing Group, Inc.
4501 Forbes Boulevard, Suite 200, Lanham, Maryland 20706
www.rowman.com

Unit A, Whitacre Mews, 26-34 Stannary Street, London SE11 4AB

British Library Cataloguing in Publication Information Available

Library of Congress Cataloging-in-Publication Data Available

ISBN 9781538115176 (electronic) | ISBN 9781538115169 (hardback : alk. paper)

♾ ™ The paper used in this publication meets the minimum requirements of American National Standard for Information Sciences Permanence of Paper for Printed Library Materials, ANSI/NISO Z39.48-1992.

Printed in the United States of America

To my students at the Columbia Secondary School for Math, Science, and Engineering in New York City and the Varga Katalin Gimnázium in Szolnok, Hungary.

# CONTENTS

# ACKNOWLEDGMENTS

I am indebted to the following individuals and organizations:

My editor at Rowman & Littlefield, Stephen Ryan, who welcomed the proposal and drafts, gave me wise advice, and saw the project through to completion; and Jessica McCleary, the production editor, who guided the words into print;

My dear friend Joyce Mandell, who read and commented on chapters of the book;

Miriam Nightengale, the principal of Columbia Secondary School, who understood and supported this project;

My relative Robert Charles Fischer, for his story about his grandfather's book prop;

Cantor Perry Fine, whose cantillation course stays in my memory and who read and commented on the fourth chapter;

Samuel Hope, executive director emeritus of the National Association of Schools of Music, for encouraging me in my work and inviting me to speak;

My colleagues at Columbia Secondary School and at the Varga Katalin Gimnázium;

My students in philosophy, language, and literature classes and all the students who shaped and filled the philosophy journal *Contrariwise*;

Dr. Nimet Küçük, who invited me to teach in May 2017 at the Sainte Pulchérie Lisesi in Istanbul;

The Dallas Institute of Humanities and Culture and the Association of Literary Scholars, Critics, and Writers for involving me in their vital work;

All those who have inspired my Jewish life and encouraged me in cantillation and more;

All my teachers, witting and unwitting;

And my friends and family, without whom I could not do.

# INTRODUCTION

We live in an era of the Big Idea (which often is not much of an idea at all): a snappy concept that appears to solve social and personal problems. A book or TED talk comes along that seems to explain everything (or at least a good chunk). People seize the takeaway, propagate it, and reduce ideas and history to fit it. I have heard people speak of "critical thinking" with uncritical admiration, about "creative disruption" as though it had released the collective genius, and about "grit" as if it gave the earth an extra push around its axis. The concept of a "team"—good for certain times and places—has come to take over all associations, all group relationships. If you suggest, at a meeting, that not everything is a team, you get a puzzled look or a sympathetic laugh. Then the meeting continues: "All right, team, let's move on to the next item." You find that a meatier (not teamier) critique is in order.

What happens when you begin questioning the language around you—not just casually, but intently? First, you can never return to it as you knew it before. Words carry grief and joy, history and impulse, help and danger. Having forayed into language, you become, in a sense, its exile. Yet this alertness to language leads to associations as well, with people who likewise question what they say and hear.

Second, you find that you must live out your questions. To question language is not simply to poke fun at it, although jokes wait in the wings. You bear the consequences of words. Clichés take over if you do not guard against them. You hear of the "bottom line," "moral imperative," "safe space," "American values," and such things; if you let them pass by without scrutiny, you will hear them again later, in louder vowels, after they have gorged on the world. You will then find it harder to get a word in edgewise, as they will crowd out every edge.

In any time—but especially in a time of memes, retweets, aggressive personalized marketing, and news gone "viral"—a skeptical, self-educating mind upholds democratic forms. Democracy requires agency; to participate in government, at any level, you must be able to work with words and grammar, construct arguments, spot fallacies, and perceive ambiguities and uncertainties. You must also respond intelligently to criticism—consider it, learn from it, and single out its wisdom. Language does not come prepackaged; to use it well, you must tousle with it, looking for the right words and combinations. It is not enough to point the finger; democratic criticism must involve full conscience. When critics seek truth, language opens its leaves. Such seeking need not take scholarly or political form; it can occur in song, technology, or reverie. It keeps pushing beyond certainty and ease, beyond its own version of the world.

From 2011 to 2016, I created and taught a sequence of philosophy courses at Columbia Secondary School in New York City. In the ninth-grade course (Rhetoric and Logic), students often asked me, "What does rhetoric have to do with philosophy?" I replied that language can help or hinder our pursuit of truth. To illustrate this, I gave an assignment. Students were to write about a concept, word, or phrase that they thought had been misused or misunderstood. In three paragraphs, they were to explain the nature of the misunderstanding, discuss the implications, and propose a different understanding or phrase. The results were so compelling that I made this an annual tradition in my classes.

Students wrote probing essays on happiness, courage, "college and career readiness," "It'll all be OK," and other expressions. Within these short compositions, possibilities multiplied and meanings grew. I came to see this as not only a useful assignment but a vital practice. Whoever peers into words becomes sharper and more skeptical of speech. For the sake of meaning, fun, and resistance, I decided to take up the same exercise in longer form. This discipline and play led to the current book.

Each chapter in this book takes up a word, phrase, or concept; criticizes its current usage; and proposes a new approach to the word or words. The chapters delve into music, literature, education, and other enduring subjects; in doing so, they take language beyond its quick rewards. To understand words well, one must hear them, not only in the moment, not only in current usage, but through time, subject matter, and solitude. One must perceive beyond the immediate present, beyond monotonic choruses of agreement and rebuke.

The title *Mind over Memes* suggests a human ability to think about the language we use instead of automatically adopting it and passing it on. The subtitle, *Passive Listening, Toxic Talk, and Other Modern Language Follies*, refers to words and phrases whose usage I critique in the book. By "follies" I mean instances of thoughtlessness, not error. Error can instruct; thoughtlessness obstructs. What John Stuart Mill wrote about truth, one can apply to language: "Truth gains more even by the errors of one who, with due study and preparation, thinks for himself, than by the true opinions of those who only hold them because they do not suffer themselves to think."[1] By thinking about language, by subjecting it to questioning, we can keep it alive.

This is not the usual habit. An unlearned hand, an insistence on being right, has taken hold of our culture. American democracy suffers not only from the current leadership (at the time of this writing, the unfortunate President Trump and his associates), but from the accusatory, dismissive, derogatory language that fills online and offline discussion. People speak not in full sentences but in clipped insults that provoke broken barbs in return. Dialogue has been reduced to reaction; Facebook, Twitter, and other platforms encourage likes, emoticons, hashtags, and mini-statements rather than serious articulation of ideas. Newspapers routinely quote from incoherent Twitter feeds. George Orwell's warnings about the English language play out daily: "It becomes ugly and inaccurate because our thoughts are foolish, but the slovenliness of our language makes it easier for us to have foolish thoughts."[2]

In a sense, this book takes up easy targets: change, creativity, the team, the takeaway—concepts so common yet so carelessly applied that they collapse at the slightest query. Yet the terms are more stubborn than they appear—partly because they have stationed themselves in daily speech, partly because they represent something needed and real. The challenge is not to banish them from the English language but to find their proper place.

Consider change: education and business reformers tend to divide humanity into two camps: the "change agents"—who courageously march toward change, whatever it might hold—and the "defenders of the status quo," who not only resist change but obstruct those who pursue it. Such proclamations and divisions make little sense. Most of us have feared, welcomed, sought out, and paused before various kinds of change; the differences lie in the particulars. To understand attitudes toward change, one must consider, among other things, just *what* change is at stake. Instead of broadcasting mantras about change, one can hold back enough to ask, "Is this true? What am I saying, and what do I mean?" This allows for wise action, as long as the questioner does not sink in self-doubt, self-righteousness, or other morasses.

Or consider creativity: What is it, and how can we support it? We hear about how it is needed, how schools and workplaces should promote it, but what does this mean, if anything? Sometimes people speak of creativity as though it consists of brainstorming sessions and ideas scribbled on Post-Its. However, if creativity involves creating something, it requires knowledge, working material, and long dedication. The ephemeral creativity often promoted in schools and workplaces may distract from larger endeavors.

Or consider trust-building (a term not discussed in this book). It has been rightly said that trust allows individuals and institutions to thrive, work together, and learn from each other. It does not follow that one can build trust through obstacle courses and get-to-know-you icebreakers. Trivialization and trust are not the same. To build trust, those involved must establish and maintain working principles, for instance, avoiding gossip and speaking frankly about problems. The leaders must establish a tone and quality of discussion.

The list of problematic words goes on. Yet criticism holds pitfalls too, such as torpor, arrogance, and excessive gravity or levity. I hope that I have avoided them in this book. Excessive uncertainty over words can lead to torpor; finding none of them adequate, one hesitates to say anything at all, or else one becomes so strained, so careful with speech, that it becomes stiff and waterlogged. This will not do; like a musician listening while playing, we must use and hear words at once, tuning ourselves as we go.

Arrogance, for its part, comes as a great temptation. Poking fun at words, we find others who have done the same, from Homer to Chesterton. We fancy ourselves part of a charmed and closed circle. This is misguided for several reasons. First, Homer and Chesterton are not looking to join a club, and if they were, they would probably have other members in mind. Second, enclosedness cannot become the goal. A book must have knowledge and conviction—an author must have something to say—but must also look outward and inward, into the larger subject and unsettled questions.

Regarding seriousness and levity, an author can go too far in either direction. A humorless, tedious book forgets that all language is a play on words.[3] On the other hand, humor is not obligatory; it must fit both the subject and the style. Seriousness, while sometimes unsettling, need not shrink from itself; it belongs in certain places. I am not John Oliver; fortunately, someone else is.

This book is not satirical, although it draws on satire. Satire ridicules something; while the chapters mock words here and there, they uphold language's meaning. In that sense, even at their proudest, they seek humility. Language tests our will; with all our vocabulary, grammar, syntax, and reading, do we dare say what we want to say, and do we know how to do it? The very difficulty suggests something at stake.

Throughout the chapters, I emphasize the importance of uncertainty—not the kind that paralyzes or confuses, but the kind that lifts us out of pat summaries. No one knows the entirety of another human or of a human condition; all our formulations are incomplete and provisional. Limiting terms—demographic, political, psychological, neurological—fly at us from many directions, yet each of us may choose whether to accept them. Each of us has the duty to call their bluff at times. Or, to quote the Constitution of Užupis (a district of Vilnius, Lithuania), "Everyone has the right to be in doubt, but this is not an obligation."[4]

I look forward to the discussions that this book will provoke. Everyone has come across the words featured in these pages; some use them daily, and some even hold them dear. Yet certain kinds of irreverence bring honor and hope.

# 1

# TAKE AWAY THE TAKEAWAY

The Problem with Pocketable Summaries

Eleven internship candidates, all high school juniors, sit in a circle. Their eyes tour the inventions in the room: a miniature air train, two robots playing chess, and a simulated stained-glass window that changes patterns and casts colored light on the floor. This engineering school showroom draws daily visitors from around the world; the candidates ask themselves in varying words, "Do I have a chance? Will I be chosen? Will this be my summer, my life?"[1]

The door slides open sideways, disappearing into the wall. All eyes follow the interviewer, who crosses to the center, sits in the remaining chair, and introduces herself as Erin Hadley. She explains the purpose of this group interview: to assess their presentation and teamwork skills. The first task will be to describe, in thirty seconds, one engineering project they completed, one challenge they overcame in the process, and one takeaway from the experience. "We really want your takeaway," she stresses.

They sit like numbers on a clock, attending the stroke of noon.

Erin calls on the first candidate, Brandon, who swiftly sums up an app he created for a parking garage. To make the program work, he says, he had to propose a minor rearrangement of the spaces; this required consultation with the management. He rolls into the takeaway: *Computer engineering requires communication and collaboration.* Erin nods, makes a mark on her sheet, and calls on Selene, who describes a program she designed to distinguish nouns from verbs. To her delight, it didn't work; the English language had far too many complexities. "It was great to find out what I had gotten myself into," she says. "Oh, right, how did I overcome this obstacle?" She hesitates. "Well, actually, I didn't," she admits, "but I learned a lot." Genial laughter breaks out.

After everyone has spoken, Erin gives them their next project: to build a shelter out of masking tape and rulers. The resulting dome, den, or other structure must hold three people and support a drape on top. They must all work together. The final stage of the interview will test their coding and problem-solving skills; they will work together to fix a bug in a simple robot program. "It's easy because time is short," she says. "The teamwork is the point."

Erin reviews her notes later and selects Brandon and two others for the position. She created the summer internship Student Entrepreneurs in Engineering (SEE) in her first year of graduate school; it has already made headlines, and she treats it with pride. She knows how easily a new program can lose focus—much like eyesight, she thinks—so she will do all she can for SEE's survival. To have the grant renewed, she will have to demonstrate success this summer.

Part of her research has been on the relationship between self-summary and success. Early on, she noticed that young engineers who could summarize their previous projects were more likely to plan and complete their current ones. This inspired the opening "takeaway task," which she hopes will become part of school curricula around the country. "If you know what you've done and what you plan to do," she likes to say, "you're already two-thirds of the way there." She now turns her eyes back to the applications.

After some hesitation, she turns Selene down. She clearly has talent but might get bogged down in complexities; she took too long explaining herself and failed to sum things up. She performed the other tasks well but did not stand out as a leader or problem-solver. *Too bad*, Erin tells herself, *but maybe she can treat this as a learning experience*. After printing out the letters, she shows them to Steven Moss, a young assistant professor heading the project. He signs them; he has already told her that he trusts her judgment.

On the surface, this outcome seems fair. An interviewee (for an internship, study program, or job) should know how to convey knowledge, experience, and insight in few words. Yet the bias toward certainty brings losses. Those who sum themselves up swiftly will be viewed as more successful—and thus more qualified for a range of opportunities—than those who take on questions and doubts. We have forgotten our Ishmael, who warns in *Moby-Dick*, "I promise nothing complete; because any human thing supposed to be complete, must for that very reason infallibly be faulty."[2] In our efforts to seem sturdy, we have dug ourselves a fault.

Our schools and culture glorify the takeaway: the pocketable answer, the successful transaction, the surety squeezed from things unsure. Originally used in business contexts, the takeaway now has a hold on education, arts, and human relations. To understand where it goes wrong, one must first consider its virtues. At its best, it helps us get things done; at its worst, it cheapens the tasks themselves. Here I will consider not only the word but the underlying phenomenon: the act of taking a complex entity and reducing it to a pat message.

By definition, a takeaway is what you "get" out of a discussion, book, or other situation. *Oxford English Dictionary* defines it (in this context) as "a key fact, point, or idea to be remembered, typically one emerging from a discussion or meeting."[3] It is the tourist trinket, the mutterable motto. Many of us can recall describing something complex—Chekhov's *Cherry Orchard*, for instance—to someone who responds, "So the takeaway is that people are scared of change, right?" If a takeaway could adequately sum up a play, you wouldn't need plays at all; a playbill would do instead.

Plays aside, sometimes a takeaway suits the occasion and saves the day. It has a place here and there. Consider a condominium association meeting. The participants move through an agenda that touches on finances, repairs, building issues, and more. It is Monday evening, and many have to get up early the next morning; they glance at their watches and worry. Last year's meeting went on for three hours with no clear resolution. But this time, after each agenda item, the moderator asks for a takeaway: a short statement of what was discussed and who will take up the problem from there. A lot gets done; someone quips that they will have to write a brand-new agenda next year. In this instance, the takeaways have lightened the load.

When applied to the wrong context, though, the takeaway reduces and distorts the subject at hand. A *New Yorker* cartoon by Mike Twohy shows a family gathered with bowed heads around a Thanksgiving table, and a man standing at the head, saying solemnly, "The takeaway tonight is 'Thanks.'"[4] The comic incongruity (between the holiday and its reduction) points to a larger cultural tendency to package up things that merit room and time. If we could reduce Thanksgiving to "thanks," we might as well reduce the meal to a turkey jerky stick. Each person could take a piece and run. Gratitude itself would be consumed and disbursed on the go.

The point is not to expel takeaways from our lives but to determine their proper bounds. The next few examples—from education, literature, and popular culture—will illustrate their overreach. Then I will propose a different approach to knowledge and questions.

School districts around the United States require teachers to set concrete, measurable goals for each lesson. This in itself should cause no outcry; many educators, parents, and students recognize the importance of specific and sequenced learning. A lesson is just one small component of that sequence; as such, it should have substance and belong to something larger. The problem arises when the objectives leave no room for the uncertain and unknown.

Teachers are frequently faulted for departing from the objective or failing to stress it repeatedly. The Dallas Independent School District's "Teacher Excellence Initiative" (the teacher evaluation system) includes the following criteria for instructional practice at the "exemplary" level:

> Without exception, effectively establishes clear and outcomes-based objectives aligned to district curriculum maps & assessments.
> Focuses students at the beginning and throughout the lesson so that all or nearly all students can clearly explain:
>
> - What they are learning beyond simply repeating back the stated or posted objective
> - Why it is important beyond simply repeating the teacher's explanation
> - What mastery looks like
> - How to connect it to prior knowledge and their own lives
> - How the objective fits into the broader unit and course goals[5]

The rigidity of this criterion ("without exception") is only part of the problem. Why make teachers reiterate the objective throughout the lesson? Is it always good to tell students in advance what they are learning and why? Must students *immediately* be able to connect the lesson to their own lives and to the larger goals of the course? That would restrict the curriculum to superficial topics; any topic worth its salt will leak through our containers. Students should come to understand the purposes of the course, but this does not require continual repetition. If you repeat the objectives over and over, you render them ridiculous.

At its best, any subject resists both sloppy and facile answers; it demands both clarity of vision and the ability to handle the unknown. In history, you must learn facts in order to look further into them (and question whether they are indeed "facts"); in literature, you come to understand a work in new ways. The play of certainty and uncertainty keeps scholars absorbed in their fields. A takeaway puts a stop to the investigation; it declares, "This is what it's all about" and shrugs off the rest.

In claiming the point, the takeaway misses the point. Student Achievement Partners' resource *Achieve the Core*, which provides materials aligned with the Common Core State Standards, offers a lesson plan that turns Robert Frost's "The Road Not Taken" into a moral lesson. It claims that the poem tells us how we should handle life decisions, when in fact it does no such thing.

"Two roads diverged in a yellow wood"—how many times have we heard or seen that opening? We think we know the poem, just as we think we know Hamlet's "To be or not to be." There are two roads in a wood; someone chooses the road "less traveled by" and realizes, years later, that this choice has "made all the difference." Yet these jaunty, melancholic verses would not have lasted, would not have ended up in anthology after anthology, had they merely commented on the virtues of unpopular choices in life. Something in the poem puzzles and teases the mind. Something refuses to rest.

First, there is a question of time, which twists and turns throughout the poem. The speaker contemplates an impossible simultaneity: "And sorry I could not travel both / And be one traveler." One cannot travel two roads as one person; one cannot even look on two roads at once or think of them at once. To be human is to be caught in time: "long I stood / And looked down one as far as I could / To where it bent in the undergrowth." That is all one can do: look down one road, then another. Or is it? In his book about this poem, David Orr comments that the speaker, looking back and forth between the two roads, creates an illusory road that is

neither the one nor the other: "The title itself is a small but potent engine
that drives us first toward one untaken road and then immediately back to
the other, producing a vision in which we appear somehow on both roads,
or neither."[6] The very contemplation makes a fiction of the roads.

Over the course of the poem—as Orr, Jay Parini, and other scholars
have observed—we find that the roads are not so different from each
other, or that the speaker cannot locate a difference with any certainty.[7] In
choosing one road, the speaker loses the other; looking back, he recalls
that he "left the first for another day" but sensed, even then, that this was
wishful thinking ("Yet knowing how way leads on to way, / I doubted if I
should ever come back"). One can understand this in various ways; even
if the speaker could return to the same geographical place, he could not
return to that same place of indecision, as the decision would already
have been made.

In the last stanza, Frost plays a crowning trick on the reader: the
speaker declares that he will "be telling this with a sigh / Somewhere ages
and ages hence"—and then tells the story that he foresees telling, a story
that contradicts what he has said so far: "Two roads diverged in a wood,
and I— / I took the one less traveled by, / And that has made all the
difference." The play of time rises to new levels; the speaker now looks
ahead to a time when he will look back to the time on which he has been
reflecting just now. From the perspective of old age, he will see the road
he took as the one "less traveled by" and will claim that his choice of road
"has made all the difference." The moral of his story, the takeaway, will
be his own fiction.

Yet the fiction may hold truth, even within the illusions of time. Perhaps what makes "all the difference" is not the choice of road but the
eventual story; perhaps "all the difference" lies in language itself. Perhaps
the road becomes "less traveled by" over time—not because fewer people
take it, but because the speaker himself, through his own walking, makes
it singular. Perhaps "all the difference" lies in those subtleties of diction
that set this poem apart from others. Within the poem, the phrase "all the
difference" wakes its twin, the cliché, out of sleep. I remember how John
Hollander, my poetry professor in college and graduate school, rumbled
those last three words. I knew then that the "difference" was not what it
seemed.

Lesson plans routinely misrepresent the poem; the one I bring up here
is no exception. On their *Achieve the Core* website, Student Achievement

Partners offer a five-day lesson plan for "The Road Not Taken." The plan begins by stating the poem's "big ideas and key understandings": that "individuals have free will to make choices that may be easy or difficult." It then summarizes the poem as follows: "The speaker reflects on the risks and responsibilities of making choices and deciding which road to take." This may seem innocuous—in some way the poem *is* about life choices—but these vague pseudo-philosophical statements oil the way for further trouble. A little later, the lesson plan offers a question: "According to the text, what is the relationship between choices in life and human beings? Use textual evidence to support your claim." It then suggests two possible answers that students might write (and that would be deemed correct):

    a.  According to the text, when making choices in life, human beings should think well about the choices they are making, "long I stood" (3). This shows that human beings should think well about the choices they are making because the text has the speaker standing long and thinking about the roads before the speaker makes a decision between the two roads. The speaker does not take another step nor choose which road between the two to take until the speaker states the words "long I stood."

    b.  According to the text, when making choices in life, human beings should acknowledge some kind of responsibility for their own choices. In the end the text states that the speaker says, "And I— /I took the one less traveled by" (18–19). This shows the speaker taking responsibility for his or her own choices. First because the speaker speaks in the first person, he or she states that he or she took the one less traveled by and not anyone else. The speaker takes ownership as the subject of the action.[8]

Something has gone wrong. Who translated this poem into a collection of "shoulds," and why? Someone must have assumed that the poem had tips and takeaways—"take time before making a decision," "take ownership of what you do"—and that, by identifying them, the students would show understanding. Some poems are indeed didactic, but this one is not. If anything, it pokes fun at the didactic. The speaker hesitates and speculates; he waffles before a decision that seems minor and then imagines a big tale he will tell one day about this decision, once it becomes part of the distant past.

The lesson plan's misreading of Frost's poem speaks to our societal desire to find a life hack, a motto, a moral in things around us. To understand the poem, one must read it on its own terms: not as a tool for finding the main idea, not as a statement about choices in life, but as verse that shakes up its own summaries. The takeaway, no longer the center of the world, rolls off into the corner. Or so runs my dream.

Takeaways have too much clout. Their dominion extends into popular culture, most notably the TED talk. If wisdom consists of learning a lot and realizing that you know little, TED feeds the desire to learn just a little and feel that you know a lot. Founded in 1984, TED (Technology, Entertainment, Design) is an American set of conferences run by the private nonprofit Sapling Foundation. The events carry the tagline, "Ideas Worth Spreading."

TED talks breathe in near-unison, "It's amazing! We can do this!" Speaker after speaker exults over a new approach to education, a path to happiness, the power of body language, the key to motivation, or some other glorious alteration of our lives.

On the surface, the spreading of ideas can only lead to good: What could be nobler than to assemble some of the world's most inspiring artists, scientists, writers, thinkers, and inventors; put them on stage; record their talks; and publish the videos online for all to see and hear? What does it matter, even, if the talks err on the simplistic side? They keep the public informed of innovations and groundbreaking concepts; they stimulate discussion and reading. Yet there is a catch: an idea must have selling power to gain the TED stage. To gain selling power, it must project warmness and inclusivity: *everyone can be part of progress*. Even the most interesting and idiosyncratic talks—by people of great accomplishment—suggest, in TED style, that anyone can take part in the genius, that it comes not from talent and hard work, or even from logical thought, but from confidence in the powers of hype.

TED's very positivity can push criticism out to the fringes. My own experience with TED illustrates the difficulty of critiquing from the inside. I was invited in April 2016 to give a talk at TEDx Upper West Side in NYC. (TEDx events are independent of TED but governed by specific TED rules.) I agreed to give the talk on the condition that I could subtly make fun of TED; the organizer approved my stipulation. In the talk I discussed the pitfalls of takeaways. With examples from algebra and *Hamlet*, I argued that the takeaway can actually detract from subject matter. I was commenting obliquely on TED talks through a TEDx Talk (a more porous and less lucrative enterprise). My talk would not have ended up on the TED stage; instead of offering an answer, it called for more uncertainty.

The most popular TED talks sell a concept and sell it hard. Most of the talks in TED's list of its "most popular talks of all time" propose an idea that supposedly will make the world better (and that does not require public expertise). Sir Ken Robinson argues for making schools more creative, Amy Cuddy for adopting "power poses" before interviews and other stressful situations, Simon Sinek for asking "Why?" (as a form of powerful leadership), Brené Brown for embracing vulnerability, Julian Treasure for speaking so that people will listen, Jill Bolte Taylor for the life guided by the right hemisphere of the brain, Tony Robbins for a method of self-actualization, Daniel Pink for the power of intrinsic motivation, Robert Waldinger on how to lead a fulfilling life, Shawn Achor on the key to work productivity, and so on. There is nothing wrong with personal and global improvement, but as the focus of TED, it undermines the larger cause of disseminating ideas. Questions and investigations get short shrift.

The most popular TED talk (in terms of hits), Robinson's "Do Schools Kill Creativity?," offers a quickly graspable idea: schools need to emphasize creativity instead of demolishing it. Robinson maintains that schools educate "from the waist up" and move toward the head as the child advances. "The whole purpose of education throughout the world," he declares, "is to produce university professors" who regard their bodies "as a form of transport for their heads." Schools, according to Robinson, need to move away from this model and respond to the needs of the age; in today's world, we have to educate the whole being, not just the brain. How should we go about this? He does not explain, except by suggesting that schools should teach dance as a serious subject. The problem lies not in his failure to get to the point; he gets to the point right away. Yet he fails to get beyond it. Nor does he acknowledge complications in his argument: for instance, the possibility that "cerebral" subjects invite intense creativity or that dance class may require cerebral discipline.[9]

While Robinson's books explain these ideas in greater detail, they do not remedy the logical flaws. In *Out of Our Minds: The Power of Being Creative*, he states that "in everyday language 'academic' is often used as a synonym for 'education'"; that is, politicians talk about "raising academic standards," as if that would improve education as a whole. Our cultural attitude toward things "academic" is mixed, he adds, yet we have created a school system whose primary purpose (as he said in his TED talk) is to "produce university professors."[10] In the following chapter, he discusses, among other things, the narrowness of university academia itself: its rigid conception of research, its expectation of conformity, and its entrenched view that some subjects are academic and others are not.[11]

All of these points both hold and omit some truth. So-called academic standards in public schools are a far cry from the practices of scholarship. Scholarship requires knowledge, insight, and versatility; in contrast, to demonstrate that they have met the "standards," students must select the correct answers on multiple-choice tests and write short essays in response to a prompt. Scholars do vastly more than that, and their work is more interesting. If schools were indeed producing university professors (or seeking to do so), we would be in better shape than we are now. But professors cannot be produced; the best go against the grain.

Robinson is right that academia has hampered scholarship—that it excludes creative endeavors, passes negative judgment on thoughtful and original work, and otherwise constrains intellectual life. This matches my own experience and the documented experience of many others (see, for instance, William Deresiewicz's *Excellent Sheep*).[12] Yet he draws his caricatures with thick charcoal (as opposed to painting with a broad brush). Within colleges and universities, there are different ways of thinking and living. Some abide by the regulations and trends, while others resist or ignore them. Some institutions seek out narrow specialties; others make room for people with unusual combinations of interests and accomplishments. I sympathize with many of Robinson's ideas but find that they sacrifice complexities to the ultimate takeaway: we need more creativity in schools.

The second-most-popular TED talk is similarly simple. Arguing that "your body language shapes who you are" (the original title, later changed to "Your Body Language May Shape Who You Are"), the social psychologist Amy Cuddy begins by promising that she will offer a "free, no-tech life hack" that asks nothing of you but "that you change your posture for two minutes." She refers to the desired posture as a "power pose"—which involves spreading the body, assuming a stance of authority, and taking space. During the talk, Cuddy describes her own 2012 study, conducted with Dana Carney and Andy Yap, which suggests that those who engage in power poses experience "elevations in testosterone, decreases in cortisol, and increased feelings of power and tolerance for risk." She concludes by advising her listeners to try the power pose.[13]

Cuddy's speech moved millions, but her study later revealed flaws. In May 2015, Joe Simmons and Uri Simonsohn analyzed the power pose study and found serious problems in it. Subsequent research by Eva Ranehill and colleagues (published in 2015) did not replicate the study's findings; to the contrary, the researchers found that power posing had no effect on hormones or risk tolerance. In September 2016, Katie Garrison and colleagues published another failed replication: they found that power posing did not influence subjects' decision to gamble; moreover, it *reduced* their feelings of power. In the same month, Carney, one of Cuddy's fellow researchers, repudiated the original study, detailed its many problems, and stated that she no longer believes that power pose effects are real. Additional studies, published in a special issue of *Comprehensive Results in Social Psychology*, suggested a small effect of power posing on feelings of power; commenting on these results in an article in the same issue, Joseph Cesario, Kai J. Jonas, and Carney cautioned against quick conclusions. While acknowledging that the testosterone hypothesis has not held up, Cuddy continues to support power pose research and to defend her own interpretations of it.[14]

While critics have focused on the study, the talk itself suffers from adherence to a TED talk format. TED upholds no single formula, but many talks, including Cuddy's, follow—or perhaps inspire—the structure that TED offers in a TEDx manual:

1. Start by making your audience care, using a relatable example or an intriguing idea.
2. Explain your idea clearly and with conviction.
3. Describe your evidence and how and why your idea could be implemented.
4. End by addressing how your idea could affect your audience if they were to accept it.

In its conclusion, the manual advises, "Find a landing point in your conclusion that will leave your audience feeling positive toward you and your idea's chances for success. Don't use your conclusion to simply summarize what you've already said; tell your audience how your idea might affect their lives if it's implemented."[15]

Cuddy began her talk by stating that she was offering a "free, no-tech life hack"; at the end of the talk, she told her audience to "share the science":

> So I want to ask you first, you know, both to try power posing, and also I want to ask you to share the science because this is simple. I don't have ego involved in this. [*Laughter*] Give it away. Share it with people because the people who can use it the most are the ones with no resources and no technology and no status and no power. Give it to them because they can do it in private. They need their bodies, privacy, and two minutes, and it can significantly change the outcomes of their life.[16]

Cuddy set out to use her findings to help others, particularly the vulnerable. She had every reason to share the conclusions of her study. But one can do this without calling them science. While not original to Cuddy, the phrase "share the science"—when it means "share the conclusions of this research"—mistakes the part for the whole. Even without knowing a study's flaws, one should keep a tentative outlook on it; it may seem to point to truth, but the investigation continues.

The study's own abstract was too rash in its takeaways; Andrew Gelman pointed out that it "concluded with a statement of something not measured in the paper," namely, "That a person can, by assuming two simple [one-minute] poses, embody power and instantly become more powerful has real-world, actionable implications."[17] The study did not measure people's actual power levels after power posing. Yet even if it could have, and even if it had, these conclusions would not constitute science. No specific conclusions *are* science; rather, they may represent a moment in a scientific process. Even less does a "life hack" qualify as science; it may appear to have scientific basis, but science is greater than basis and hack together.

TED's prevailing style discourages questions and doubt. Analyzing TED's popularity, Nathan Heller asks, "Why speak rigorously to an audience of hundreds when you can ham it up a bit and spread the fruits of your research to millions?" The popularity of TED, he posits, is due at least in part to its emotional appeal: "TED may present itself as an ideas conference, but most people seem to watch the lectures not so much for the information as for how they make them feel." Alex Pareene identifies four common tropes of TED talks: "drastically oversimplified explanations of complex problems"; "technologically utopian solutions to said complex problems"; "unconventional (and unconvincing) explanations of the origins of said complex problems"; and "staggeringly obvious observations presented as mind-blowing new insights." TED has capitalized on a larger cultural tendency and, in doing so, has exacerbated it. A TED talk now serves as a ticket to a book contract, a speaking tour, and more. "TED talks have become a rite of passage for thought leaders," writes Jason Kehe in *Wired*. "You're an expert in your field, and it's time to tell the world." He offers a formula for TED success, which includes a "statement of utter certainty." "People come for answers," he says; "give 'em what they want, as Shawn Achor did: 'By training your brain . . . we can reverse the formula for happiness and success.'" He also suggests a contrarian thesis, a story of personal failure, a snappy refrain, and several other touches. TED is not a place for pondering, it seems.[18]

This penchant for quick and "hot" answers goes far beyond TED; it has affected scholarship itself. Gelman and Kaiser Fung comment that "the weakest work with the boldest claims often attracts the most publicity, helped by promotion from newspapers, television, websites, and bestselling books."[19] Yet cautious certainty also receives rewards. Science research grants tend to go to projects with strategic value (such as nanotechnology) and a prespecified outcome. This influences research; when designing projects, researchers will consider the likelihood of obtaining funding. According to the editors of *Scientific American*, most scientists today must fund their laboratories and even their salaries with grant money; in response to the demand for funds, agencies tend to favor proposals with greater certainty of short-term success. "Inundated with proposals," they write, "agencies tend to favor worthy but incremental research over risky but potentially transformative work."[20] In other words, they want to know what they are getting—and thus may limit what gets asked, pursued, and accomplished. Or else the researchers work around the system, crafting confident, snazzy proposals but working on different problems altogether. Either way, the system makes people wary of inquiry, especially the kinds that lead we know not where.

A takeaway has the pack and puff of a package. It may or may not contain anything—but it looks like a "thing," as the expression goes. Quick opinion is the new coinage; we are expected to sum up everything we encounter. If we do not have words, we can click a rating. The pressure to do so is incessant; after almost every performance I attend, restaurant I visit, or purchase I make, I receive a survey to fill out. We have erected nonstop factories of chatter and evaluation.

To find examples, one need only look at reviews of *Hamlet* (Folger edition) on Amazon. Some of the more recent reviews read, "Spoiler alert: Everyone dies"; "It is great"; "Not my favorite Shakespeare book, but it's a classic if you like Shakespearean tragedy, which I do"; "excellent"; and so on. These comments (mixed with some thoughtful and thorough reviews) add nothing to readers' knowledge or understanding; they could just as well not exist, except that their authors felt compelled to say something. If you have not given your opinion, it seems, you have not done your part. (If, on the other hand, you put thought and care into your words, you risk speaking to no one.)

When asked to complete a survey of a concert or play I have just attended, I find myself in a quandary. On the one hand, I want to support the production (if it is good). On the other, I find that I may shortchange the performance by commenting on it too soon. I have often gone to performances alone so that I wouldn't have to talk; the more the event matters to me, the more silence I may need around it. Of course reviews of a performance play an important role; for instance, they can inspire others to go see it. Yet reviewers and commentators abound; no shortage seems likely in the near future. In contrast, the act of pausing has become rarer.

Yet sometimes a fad goes to such extremes that people cry out for a pause. In September 2015, Nicole McCullough and Julia Cordray announced plans for their new app, Peeple, through which people could rate individuals on the basis of their personal, professional, and romantic relationships. The announcement met with outcry and derision; many took it as a hoax, while others jeered it as one of the worst ideas to hit the Internet. (John Oliver commented on his satirical news show *Last Week Tonight*, "That sounds absolutely awful.") In response to the deluge of angry comments, the founders modified the original prospectus for the app; now only those who registered could be reviewed, and the review would be published only after the reviewee had approved it.[21]

The product launched quietly in March 2016; according to reports, its existing version is tamer than the original proposal.[22] Two years later, there was nary a peep from Peeple. This suggests that whatever the reductive forces of culture and technology, people will ultimately defend their dignity. But subtle and blatant reduction persists and prospers. The people may protest Peeple but readily accept other reductions of humanity: personality tests, hashtags, status updates, likes, followers, and online "outing" and shaming.

A takeaway culture turns ideas, works, and people into disposable items. It creates a plethora of topic sentences without real topics. It shuts out things that require thought and time. To mesh with this environment, people must be swift and glib. Misfits, those whose words do not fit the template, get ignored.

Judgment itself is not the culprit. We live by our judgment; through it, we distinguish good from bad, safe from dangerous, kind from mean, wise from foolish. In addition, we make provisional judgments for our own sanity ("Mr. X may be wise and kind, but he bugs me, and I do not wish to be his friend."). There is no such thing as a "nonjudgmental" attitude; every act, every word involves a judgment of some kind. Yet it is possible to make judgments while recognizing their limitations and errors, subjecting them to doubt, and changing them over time.

To give takeaways their proper place, one must engage in perceptive and disciplined work—not just "hard" work but engagement with a vast subject, be it music, a language, mathematics, a literary work, or a person. Infinity can be a bit much, so one must break it down—but without mistaking the pieces for the whole. It is possible, now and then, to sit with something one does not understand: to watch a play in an unknown language, read a math book far above one's level, attend an advanced physics lecture, or recognize that others, too, have thoughts, struggles, and wishes. Yet this is not the answer to the takeaway problem; there is no single answer, no three steps to follow, no two minutes guaranteed to change a life.

If there were, one could fight takeaway with takeaway; there would be a takeaway showdown one glorious afternoon, and the winning takeaway would claim the world. To see beyond takeaways, one must have prudence and discernment. One must figure out when to work gradually at a task and when to plunge in, when to take on great difficulty and when to relax into ease, when to speak and when to hold back. But a life made only of decisions would be frantic; they exist for the sake of something else.

I return to the high school students in the fictional interview room. How many of them imagined that the internship would lift up their lives; how many of us have similar dreams? We want to be chosen, elected, recognized—yet all of this exists at different levels. Throughout our lives, we select people and things; we form friendships, find interesting studies and jobs, and choose how to spend free time. Stamps of recognition, status, or identity—best-selling author, Yale student, TED speaker—do not have the last say; they may or may not come to us, but in the meantime, we continue to perceive, seek out, and choose.

To choose something is to treat it as worthy of attention. Through gaze and thought, the worth keeps changing into more. "Worth" may derive from the proto-Indo-European *wert-, "to turn, wind." Like clocks and wells, but with mind, we continue winding and turning—learning new things, pausing over them, and returning to the old. Bare in the wind and the whirling, we ask ourselves, each alone, "What if I was wrong all along?" Takeaways fall to the ground, but the question holds up; once the rain passes, it glitters in the light, and when the night comes, it keeps guard. No takeaway can light a candle to this trembling monument.

# 2

# CHANGE, OUR FALSE GOD

## Questioning the Rhetoric of Reform

**Y**ears ago, when I worked in the catalog department of a university library, a change consultant came to speak to the staff. We had begun replacing the card catalog with an online database; some catalogers welcomed this change, while others worried about their jobs and the future of the library. To head off some of the rumbling, the library management devoted a training session to the topic of change itself. The consultant, who seemed a traveler from a newfangled land, began by giving us a change readiness questionnaire.

To my amusement, many of the questions had to do with purchasing and vacation habits: How often did I buy new shoes? A new car? When going on vacation, did I like to return to the same place each year or to try out new places? I found the questions both puzzling and revealing; they apparently associated *buying* with openness to change. (Why make such an association? Might there not be inventors—for instance, astrophysicists—who get steeped in their work and forget about their shoes? Likewise, might not some people spend so much money and time on shoes that they hesitate to walk anywhere in them?) While I may have misunderstood the purpose of the questionnaire, and while I remember it only dimly now, I enjoyed the puzzlement it brought. From that day onward, I was changed; I began questioning common notions of change.

The questioning continues, along with research and introspection. The clichés continue as well. At least once a week I hear a version of one of these statements:

"People don't like change."

"We have to keep up with the times."

"Watch for those defenders of the status quo."

In business, politics, and education, these mottoes fill the daily discourse. Yet they come from mistaken assumptions: (1) that change is inevitable and ubiquitous; (2) that it can be divorced from stability; and (3) that it has some kind of edge over stability. Behind all of these is the fantastical notion (4) that one can discuss change in the abstract at all. I will examine these four assumptions, take up the three mottoes one by one, and propose a sounder conception of change.

Is change really inevitable and ubiquitous? We have heard Heraclitus's famous statement *panta rhei* ("all things change"), but it needs a counterbalancing truth. We rely on stability; our lives would make no sense without it. A piano gradually falls out of tune but otherwise keeps its shape, location, and function. If it were to grow a fourth pedal or wobble its way into the kitchen, you and I might shriek and run out the door. Whoever sits down at the piano for daily practice expects, first of all, that this will be the same piano as yesterday and, second, that it will be essentially piano-like. The tone may change over time, the pitches may go askew, but a certain piano-ness will prevail. Thousands of things offer this kind of stability, even as they change. This holds true not only for objects but for humans and organizations. If my teeth are in good shape, I can predict, with some confidence, that I will have as many tomorrow as I do today.

In 2003, the scholars Andrew Sturdy (then at Imperial College, London) and Christopher Grey (then at Cambridge University) published a sharp and rousing article with the dull title "Beneath and Beyond Organizational Change Management: Exploring Alternatives." They begin by quoting an imaginary text, which I present here in excerpted form:

> We live in a world of unprecedented stability. Technology continues to shape how we communicate, travel, work and live. . . . Those organizations where change is attempted usually fail in their efforts (66% according to one estimate) or achieve only marginal effects. Some disappear altogether as competition ensures that such failures prove costly in time and effort. *It is therefore imperative that today's managers*

*embrace stability and learn to manage continuity if they want to survive.*

This passage excepted, I never hear talk of "a world of unprecedented stability," but it seems just as plausible as "a world of unprecedented change." The authors comment: "The extent to which this fictitious quotation seems amusing, paradoxical, ridiculous or simply wrong is a testament to the solidity of the power effects of discourses of change and change management in organization studies and related fields. Yet it is, in our view, no less sustainable than the mass of hyperbole arguing the opposite."

By challenging the language surrounding change, Sturdy and Grey (terrific names) open up new possibilities for combinations of change and continuity. They begin by pointing out that continuity exists—not just as "a problem or a nullity," but as a state "coexistent and coterminous" with change. "If change is not inevitable and desirable," they write, "but contingent and contested, then the organizational and political consequences are potentially profound."[1]

What would happen if people viewed change and stability as "coexistent and coterminous"? To begin with, a given change would require integrity to execute. It would be subject to deliberation and scrutiny; no one would have to accept it just because it was *new* or because everyone else was adopting it. In addition, it would involve some kind of stability (for its own good and the good of those affected). Suppose a software company has learned that other companies are replacing offices and cubicles with open work spaces. Instead of jumping into this change because it was out there in the world, the company could consider whether it would actually enhance the work and atmosphere. To what extent do programmers need quiet and seclusion? To what extent do they need to have their colleagues within speaking range? By considering the nature of the work itself, the company could determine the optimal layout.

Similarly, a college might learn that other educational institutions were undergoing a "rebranding" process to make themselves more attractive to students and donors. This college could consider whether such rebranding was worth the thousands of dollars spent on a new color scheme, logo, or font. After carefully considering the possible benefits and losses, the college could decide whether to pursue this course of action or direct the funds elsewhere. Either way, it would not succumb to the pressure to go along with the latest trend. The rebranding movement would have no more power over the college than a balloon over a coliseum.

Even in personal matters, a sense of both change and continuity can bring clarity. When I was in seventh grade, I wanted intellectual challenge but found it in none of my classes. I brought this up with the school counselor, who said that the junior high school years were time for socializing and that I should relax. He did not consider the possibility that intellectual challenge could help a young person form social bonds. When I transferred to a private school in Boston, I began to thrive in studies of French, Latin, literature, history, algebra, music, and other subjects; I found friendships that have lasted to this day. It is through thinking about something that we learn who we are; if we were to dwell on our changes, and nothing but our changes, we would find ourselves gazing into the thick swarm of self, waiting vainly for a hint of shape.

Change and stability cannot even be separated from one another; they exist in continual relation. It is impossible to describe a change without some stable referent. Even Heraclitus's ever-changing river must have some recognizable attributes of a river, or the change would become pure chaos (which, as chaos, would lack change). Change depends on some structure for definition; even if this structure also changes, some aspect remains intact.

Examples of this combination can be found in publishing. Some believe the book will soon be obsolete, given the rise of e-books and other digital formats. Yet these technological changes draw out the book's distinguishing features. People turn to the book for what it uniquely offers: pages to turn, things to read in tranquility (without pop-up ads), personal copies that bear the marks of the owner, and so on. As a result, many e-books have imitated features of actual books (such as page turning, underlining, and shelf location). The technological changes have actually demonstrated the book's endurance.[2]

In life as well as in books, change contains some kind of continuity; the two may be entwined. The lawyer who becomes a teacher may maintain her regard for logic; the teacher who becomes an athlete may find stamina through thought. The one who says "You've changed" to a friend or partner may worry that, in fact, the other has *not* changed—that these emerging qualities were there all along. Change and stability combine intricately; sometimes a change has a constancy behind it, and sometimes a seeming change is just a rearrangement, an emergence of hidden things into the foreground.

Now let us consider the assumption that change is inherently good (and superior to stability). This has both logical and ethical problems.

People often claim that new technology aligns us with the needs of the twenty-first century and thus allows us to succeed within it. If you are on the side of the good, therefore, you will want to get new technology into the hands of every schoolchild in America. The organization One Laptop per Child explains its mission:

> We aim to provide each child with a rugged, low-cost, low-power, connected laptop. To this end, we have designed hardware, content and software for collaborative, joyful, and self-empowered learning. With access to this type of tool, children are engaged in their own education, and learn, share, and create together. They become connected to each other, to the world and to a brighter future.[3]

Stories of failed laptop initiatives aside, this statement contains its own deceptions. Why assume that a laptop, even one loaded with educational software, will promote "collaborative, joyful, and self-empowered learning"? Even if the laptops and Internet connections are in perfect working order (conditions not to be assumed), a laptop can offer only what it has. It enables certain kinds of collaboration but not others; it does not guarantee joy or any other emotional state. Children reading online about violence, receiving their first nasty comment, or even waiting for slow pages to load might experience anything from frustration to distress. In the meantime, they may miss out on learning, collaboration, and joy.

As for self-empowered learning (supposedly another feature of the laptop), this too has benefits and drawbacks. If I wish to learn kayaking, I can perhaps gain some useful tips from videos, but I will not learn until I get in the water and start rowing. The laptop empowers me only up to a point. If I wish to study Hebrew, I can find many resources online but will also need to practice alone and with others. I will need people in my life who know the language deeply and can point out its subtleties. Even adaptive software—which supposedly allows students to learn at their own pace—has limitations; it does not compare to a teacher who looks at the subject from different angles and poses surprising questions.

A laptop offers some resources but not others; before purchasing a laptop for every child, one should consider what it will and will not offer, what infrastructure and other support it requires, and what place it occupies in education. To sidestep these questions, or to treat them as secondary, is to confuse and obfuscate the language of change.

Towering above all change fallacies is the notion that there can be a general theory of change or that people do or don't like change overall. This makes no sense; change is inherently varied. To discuss it at all, one must look at its particulars. Is it natural change, willed change, or a combination? What exactly is being changed, and why? What are the choices and possible losses? Specifics take work; an analysis and careful discussion of a *particular* change may slow down the change itself. Yet this slowness can strengthen and enrich the change. The strongest innovator (or "change agent") may be the one who rejects the temptations of rush, fashion, and vagueness.

Let us now examine each of the three sayings about change that I quoted at the outset: "People don't like change"; "We have to keep up with the times"; and "Watch for those defenders of the status quo."

Word has it that people don't like change, that we are "creatures of habit." Is this true? First, we must clarify what kind of change we mean. For the sake of simplicity, we can look at three levels of individual habit and change: (a) daily routines; (b) underlying conditions (our location, relationships, and job); and (c) internal life, including ideas, religious beliefs, affections, political leanings, and tastes.

Daily routines have great variety and range. Some people take the same route to work every day; others vary it deliberately (this may depend on their time constraints and the safety of the routes). Some take walks, day after day, along the same paths; others explore something different each time. But beware: those who take the same paths every day may notice something different with each iteration. There may be profound changes within an apparent routine. By the same token, there may be sameness within apparent novelty; the person who *always* takes new paths is committed to a routine of selecting the route, making sure it is new, and so on.

Underlying conditions affect our relationship with change. Suppose, for instance, that you have been working in Boston for ten years but are now asked to move with your firm to Chicago. Your "liking" for this kind of change will probably depend on an array of circumstances. If your decision affects no one else, it may depend on how much Chicago appeals to you (and what you know about it), what kind of relocation assistance you will receive, and what your other prospects are. Some may find it exciting, even exhilarating, to move to a new city. Your spouse's and children's reactions will likely emanate from their circumstances: how attached they are to their local surroundings, institutions, and friends and how much the new place appeals to their imagination and practical sense. Even there, people can surprise themselves. Those who resist the move may find themselves thrilled with the Windy City; those who embrace it may later yearn for Rhode Island.

Or what about a change that involves not a geographical move but a shift to a different way of life within the same place? Suppose, for instance, that you have had a ritual of meeting with a particular friend, once a week, for conversation and perhaps a concert or play. Then, for one reason or another, the friend becomes unavailable. You have no comparable ritual with anyone else. Many would dislike such a change, but not because it *is* change; rather, the loss of a friend is at stake.

In contrast, perhaps you have been kept up at night, for years, by booming music coming from down the street. Polite requests to turn the stereo down, even calls to the police, have resulted in nothing. Then, one day, for reasons you do not know, the music stops and does not come back. There is music now and then on the street—but not the kind that shakes the walls and floors. Unless you enjoy being kept up at night by massive thumping sounds, you probably "like" this change toward quiet. Once again, it is the content of the change that matters. On the other hand, if you later learn that the beat-thumping neighbor had fallen ill, you might feel some sadness as well.

When it comes to changes within an individual, the picture becomes still more complex. We can delight in some aspects of a change (a new understanding of a book, for instance) while resisting other aspects (the discovery of our own errors and misunderstandings). Any given change can bring excitement, pain, confusion, and clarity, sometimes all at once or in close succession.

When I was fourteen, spending a year in Moscow (with my family), I proudly recited a Nikolai Nekrasov poem in literature class. When the teacher questioned me about it, I gave my interpretation only to hear a sharp "Nyet." At the time, I thought that she was being dogmatic. A few years later, when rereading the poem and remembering the incident, I saw that I had actually misunderstood the interrogative particle "li" in the poem—and, with that, the entire meaning. I saw that my interpretation was incorrect, not just different from hers. This affected my view not only of the poem but of teaching poetry; I realized that there *were* right and wrong interpretations, along with open questions. The two-letter "li" had opened into poetry itself. I was embarrassed about the error and in that sense "didn't like change" (since to see one's own error is to change). Still, what I learned became more and more important over time.

Thus, when evaluating the statement "People don't like change," one must ask, first, what order of change it is; second, what it contains; and third, what kind of "liking" is involved. Some changes are quite appealing; others understandably bring discomfort. People may well embrace or resist certain kinds of changes, but their responses may have layers. Often what matters is not so much what they "like" as how they work with their choices and constraints.

Let us now proceed to the second statement: "We have to keep up with the times." What are the times, and is it true that one should "keep up with them"? Our time, anyone's time, consists of a layer of times. At any moment we may draw on ideas and works from centuries ago; at any moment we may break away from a current trend. There is no reason to equate the "times" with whatever happens to be "trending"; this is perilous in fact. We are part of our times by definition; we do not need to scramble to stay on their conveyor belt. If keeping up means conforming automatically, then there is good reason to stop and think.

Any time is a mixture of times. My bookshelf has Homer and Will Self; the Homer (*Iliad* and *Odyssey*) contains an array of time periods, including those of transcription, translation, editing, publishing, and many readings. A translator works with a mixture of times; he or she must decide when to keep the sense and form of the original (insofar as it is known) and when to render it in contemporary terms and sounds. In their translations of the *Iliad*, Richmond Lattimore and Robert Fagles bring old and new together in different ways: "Sing, goddess, the anger of Peleus' son Achilleus" and "Rage—Goddess, sing the rage of Peleus' son Achilleus."[4] The one emphasizes singing, the other rage; both bring the sound of the ancient Greek (or some imagining of it) into English words. The Self (as in Will) seems to occupy a narrower range of times, but its strange, sharp humor goes to the belly of all laughter. Humor is often local and contextual—but laughter itself cuts through time and culture.

Inside and outside books, we lead our lives by bringing together past, present, and future. A conversation with a friend might involve not only "catching up" (what has happened since we saw each other last?) but also *not* catching up—that is, enjoying each other's company right then and there. In the classroom, a teacher may respond both to the immediate comments and to memories of comments made years ago, while thinking ahead to the next point in the lesson. A Broadway production of *Fiddler on the Roof* involves historical memory, memory of past productions, memory of the morning rehearsal, and many other kinds of memories, all combined with immediacy and anticipation. Our most important actions involve complex combinations of memory, spontaneity, and foresight.

Our times, then, go far beyond the here and now; they essentially consist of all times. To keep up with the times, in the best sense of the word, is to draw on an understanding of history. This may require resisting trends. When one's best judgment clashes with the current fashion, then this judgment should gain the upper hand. Unfortunately, when people speak of "keeping up with the times," they often mean conforming and giving in.

What about the admonition "Watch for the defenders of the status quo"? This often comes from self-proclaimed reformers in education and business. They assume that those who resist a particular reform are trying to keep things in a state of poverty, mediocrity, or decline. Things are obviously more complicated than that; sometimes people resist a reform because it is flawed and one-sided, because its implementation is heavy-handed, or because its proponents do not listen to critics. Instead of dismissing critics as "defenders of the status quo," one should consider what they have to say. Perhaps the reform in question needs more careful planning and thought; perhaps it need not completely replace the existing structures.

In a speech at the first annual Teach For America Alumni Awards and Educators Conference, TFA co-CEO Elisa Villanueva Beard declared that "the enemy is the status quo" and that "for those who defend it—the burden of proof is on them to explain to the parents of America's poorest children why it's better to do nothing than something." Later, in an opinion piece, she explained her use of the term:

> Defenders of the status quo include those who aren't outraged by the
> fact that low-income children lag far behind their more affluent peers,

even though we know something else is possible. It also includes those who dismiss the real and measurable progress we're seeing in good traditional public and charter schools simply because of ideological opposition to a particular model of school reform. Defenders of the status quo include those who spend more time criticizing those who are working to tackle this deeply entrenched problem than they do working for positive change.[5]

Beard makes a few assumptions that do not hold up under scrutiny. First, she assumes that a person must be "outraged" about economic inequalities in order to qualify as an honest supporter of school reform. This is not so; while teaching requires intention and intensity, these take different forms from teacher to teacher. Not everyone focuses primarily on social justice (as it is commonly conceived). Second, she suggests that ideological opposition is disconnected from the reality on the ground; this is sometimes but not always true. The last assertion—that defenders of the status quo "spend more time" criticizing others' efforts to improve schools than they do "working for positive change"—presumes that criticism is not inherently positive and that critics are doing nothing. Granted, some criticism amounts to scratching the air, but other forms can save schools much waste and grief.

The status quo, moreover, may have more than one quality at once. Any school, even a troubled school, may have outstanding courses, praiseworthy traditions, and wise teachers. Before replacing the entire curriculum or adopting a new pedagogical model, those involved should carefully examine what is there. The danger lies not in throwing out the "baby" with the bathwater, but in sweeping out the old sages with the dust. In many cases, the status quo can strengthen and inform innovation.

Overall, the phrase "defenders of the status quo" confuses the issues and should be replaced with a more precise description of the reforms at stake, the criticisms, and their patterns of convergence and divergence.

If our conception of change is so limited, what might be offered in its place?

The dictionary offers some clues. The word "change" possibly derives from the proto-Indo-European root *kemb-*, meaning "to bend, crook." When bent, an object retains its material composition but changes its shape; in bending, therefore, there is both stability and change. By the time it reached Latin (*cambire*), the word had acquired the sense of "to exchange, barter"; in its Anglo-Norman form, *chaunge*, and in the Old and Middle French *change*, it referred to some kind of reciprocal trade (such as the exchange of prisoners in warfare). Exchange has a sort of permanence, like the conservation of energy: you trade one thing for another, but both things remain. Only later did the word "change" acquire a sense of transformation from one state into another, thus approximating the meaning of "mutate."[6]

"Mutate" is more drastic in meaning, carrying connotations of both alternation and transformation. It may derive from the proto-Indo-European root *\*mei-*, "to change, go, move," possibly the source of the Avestan *mithos,* "perverted, false"; the Latin *meare* means "to go, pass" (like the Russian *minovat'*). Other descendants of *\*mei-* connote exchange; the Latin *mutuus,* "done in exchange," and *communis,* "in common," come from the same root. By the mid-fifteenth century, the French *mutation* had the sense of "revolt"; a century later, it came to refer to alterations in the physiology of a species.[7] In current usage, "change" is more conservative than "mutate"; one can change while retaining identifying features. "You've changed" does not signify "You've grown an extra nose." It means, rather, "You are behaving somewhat differently within your existing form." Thus to "change" is implicitly to stay somewhat the same.

Change confronts us with oppositions. It involves both natural processes and human decisions; it combines with various kinds of stability. Thus, when considering a particular change, one can approach it richly.

It takes more than a lifetime, more than thousands of lifetimes, to find the right attitude toward change. It takes more than wisdom, more than knowledge, more than insight. All the same, we can move toward understanding, refining it over time. This requires accepting that we are always somewhat wrong, that our judgments may improve but can never reach perfection. Still, we make profound changes through subtle correction.

Study is fundamental to any rational change; when considering and planning a change, we should know what we are doing. Study requires a certain withholding of movement (though it has movements of its own). To change without succumbing to trends, to preserve what merits preserving, we must take time to consider the underlying subjects and questions. A practice of study will guide and shape the effort.

Let us define study broadly as a persistent and structured movement toward understanding. One might study an engine, a face, or a magnetic field. Such study forces us to put ourselves in perspective. To devote

ourselves to study, we must set aside our immediate urges and preoccupations; to do that, we must recognize their limitations. The world and our
appetites can often wait. Study involves resisting many pulls; in this
sense, it requires not only stability but staunchness.

It requires strong humility as well. To understand something, we must
face our mistakes and misconceptions. Instead of condemning ourselves,
we can take heart in the improved understanding. The error may be interesting; it may open up a subject of its own. In any case, study allows a
person to shed arrogance and find a proper relation to the problem at
hand.

Study also strengthens integrity; giving a subject our full attention, we
find who we are against it. Integrity is that sturdy, gray part of the self
that does not bend to fads, pressure, or even internal passion. As Flannery
O'Connor suggests, it takes its form because it cannot do otherwise.[8] As
it takes hold, it shakes away its overcoat, cuts its excess words, and
speaks clearly. Integrity is not static; over time, a person learns when and
how to say "no."

Sometimes change, by casting away unneeded forms, reveals what
was there all along. As individuals and organizations, we often change
into sameness. Through pursuing our work, coming to know ourselves
and others, and taking up questions, we find something recognizable in
the whirl. Knowing it, we can take it in new directions. Neither change
nor stasis is the enemy or hero; rather, the main enemies are jargon and
hype, the belief that because a change is afoot, everyone must adopt it,
and anyone who resists is a fearful fuddy-duddy, cringing in the corners
of modernity.

The concept of change needs changing, but let us not get carried away;
a total overhaul of change will change nothing. To view change more
richly, we can treat it as a mixture of things, then contemplate and work
with the mix. Instead of dividing the room into heroes and villains—
"change agents" and "change resisters"—we (together and separately)
can regard changes from different angles and look for wise action. A
thousand miles of jargon cannot compare to a cubic pinch of prudence.

# 3

# THE UBIQUITOUS TEAM

## Not Everything Has to Be One

To start off, I offer olive branches and pizza to colleagues who say "Good morning, team" and similar things. Clearly you mean cheer and respect. Yet I wonder why some say "team" with gusto while others gulp at the word. I wonder also why nearly every kind of association is called a team today; this was not always so. The words matter; they help us define our relationships and endeavors. They affect our humors too; a misplaced term like "team" catches the mind in the twine of a basketball hoop.

I am one of the gulpers. I find less wiggle room on the team than in the ensemble, association, or friendship. In those groupings, I can speak for myself and bring my best to the endeavor; on a team, I see a ball whizzing my way and know that I must catch it (or else "miss the ball," as it were). The team does not encourage contemplation, hesitation, or strong difference. As one of many kinds of relations, it can do good; sadly, it has steamrolled (or "teamrolled") its way into hubris. We have become over-teamed.

I admit to initial biases and fears. From childhood I have quailed at teamwork. I had trouble with team sports, especially those that demanded quick reflexes. Even in music camp, among dreamers, I stood out like an elbow; when we played volleyball on weekends, I would hear the others cry out, "She's from outer space!" because I was thinking about something other than the ball. I enjoyed thinking on my own; this became part of my strength. From those years onward, teams and I kept a respectful distance, for the most part. Later, when teams took over all walks of life, I questioned and lampooned my way through them, as did others. The teams were louder than their critics, though, so I fancied myself alone.

Later, in my studies and teaching, I discovered people who, like me, questioned the team's ubiquity. In 1990 Margaret Buchman wrote of the dignity and inwardness of the teachers' daily work:

> There is no paradox in claiming that some forms of inwardness, of "being situated within," are consistent with improving teaching and schools, although the idea of teachers pottering around in their classrooms, putting things into working order, and making small-scale changes may be unpalatable to outsiders given to grander schemes and prior images of human agency. Yet it does not follow that what is grander in scope or style, and higher in status, is also more appropriate, good, or right. Conversely, the potterers may be looking at the stars. [1]

In 1993 the education scholars Mieke Clement and Katrine Staessens pointed to a "fundamental difference between a team of football players and a team of teachers":

> The core events in the two professions differ entirely in nature. For a football team, the core event is a collective event: a football game. Of course, the individual players have to be well trained for this collective event. The core event for a team of teachers is what happens in the classroom between teacher and pupils. This is not a collective event, although teachers can benefit from good collegial relations and support. By denying this state of affairs, one denies the fundamental nature of teaching and being a teacher.

Yet team language has overtaken education despite the poor fit. The trend, which began at some point in the 1990s, has now peaked. It is even taboo today to suggest that a teacher's work has solitary aspects; the team has encompassed everything. "Good teachers are team players," the visible and invisible banners declare. Few dare to suggest that excellence also comes from solitude or that collaboration itself requires introspection. [2]

Thirty years ago, the "team" descriptor was generally reserved for entities that entered group competitions. There was a soccer team, a debate team, and so forth. Occasionally one might hear of a research team, but "research group" was more common. Then, without any public discussion of the matter, the word "team" took over. English departments (at least in K–12 education) became English teams. Editorial boards became editorial teams. Choral teams, poetry teams, and spiritual teams started to pop up. The word walked through our sleep unchecked. It is now time to question the phantom.

What is a team? The word derives from the Old English *team*, "descendant, family, race, line; child-bearing, brood; company, band; set of draft animals yoked together," which in turn may derive from the proto-Indo-European *\*douk-mo-*, from root *\*deuk-*, "to lead."[3] *Oxford English Dictionary* gives numerous definitions of teams, including "a family or brood of young animals"; "a set of draught animals"; "two or more beasts, or a single beast, along with the vehicle which they draw"; and (more to the point here) "a number of persons associated in some joint action; now *esp.* a definite number of persons forming a side in a match, in any team sport; hence, a group collaborating in their professional work or in some enterprise or assignment."[4]

All of these definitions connote compulsion and conformity. A "brood of young animals" exists not through free association but through the bond of common birth. Animals yoked to a vehicle have not voluntarily undertaken this enterprise. Even the looser sense of the word, "a number of persons associated in some joint action," suggests some kind of tightly coordinated work. While not obligated to join, you must submit to the common goal once you do. The grasses are not yours to roam—not that they were before, but now you must give over even the mental cattails and rye.

Shakespeare used the word "team" once each in six plays and one poem, always with the sense of "a set of draught-animals": "By the triple Hecate's team" (*A Midsummer Night's Dream*), "He that ears my land spares my team" (*All's Well That Ends Well*), "The hour before the heavenly-harnessed team / Begins his golden progress in the east" (*Henry IV, Part I*), "Drawn with a team of little atomies" (*Romeo and Juliet*), "but a team of horse shall not pluck that from me" (*The Two Gentlemen of Verona*), "The fore-horse in the team, or I am none / That draw i'th' sequent trace" (*The Two Noble Kinsmen*, attributed to John Fletcher and William Shakespeare), and "Wishing Adonis had his team to guide" (*Venus and Adonis*).[5] These quotes draw attention to the distinction between the team and the leader; the former serves the latter, and the latter is endowed with speech. Even the fairies in *A Midsummer Night's Dream* are not part of a team; they may run alongside the team but are free of its yoke. Only the quote from *The Two Noble Kinsmen* suggests that the speaker *could* be part of a team, but even there, he would only be the "fore-horse." Anything else would jeopardize his free will.

Even in current usage and practice, a team subordinates the individual to a specific group goal or outcome. A soccer team may have outstanding players, but its purpose is to win against the opposing team—even as it has the crowd gasping at its plays. A player's powerful kick counts for nothing unless it results in a goal (or prevents the other team from scoring). In a workplace, a team is supposed to get things done, not question the premises of the work itself. Those who perform the requisite tasks, in coordination with others, will be considered good "team players."

The word must offer something that people want, or it would not have taken over. People probably do not think in terms of being yoked to a vehicle; some other sense of the word attracts them. What could it be? Although baffled, I will offer some possibilities. First, the team is the entity that gets things done, almost by definition. Just as it would be strange for a religious leader to ask the congregation, "So, did we accomplish our worship goals today?" so it would be out of place for a team leader *not* to ask an analogous question. A team must have a task, or it might as well disband. So a team offers possible group accomplishment and satisfaction. If you join a team, be it a robotics team, a cycling team, or a dry-cleaning team, you can expect to complete something together, provided the team functions as it should.

In addition, a team can offer respite from selfishness on the one hand and personal responsibility on the other. Members of a team may feel gratified to serve others and be part of a shared endeavor. (The team itself may have selfish goals; I will discuss that later.) Also, the *individual* team members typically do not have to make difficult decisions; they get approval simply for doing their share of the work and taking part in group decisions. Doubt, agony, and ambivalence subside; the outward work replaces the internal struggle. Many welcome this state of things, and why not? Is it not better to work with others and get things done than to harp on life's vagaries and vicissitudes? "Get out of your own head," common sense advises, "and join with others." The slogan "There's no 'I' in 'team'" comes to some as a relief.

A team offers not only accomplishment and respite from self, but also continual pep and cheer. Just as cheerleaders chant and dance to encourage football teams, so teams themselves act as their own champions, erupting every so often with "Go, team!" When a team achieves a goal, it can expect praise from within and without: "Fantastic teamwork! Let's hear it for the team!" This is no accident but rather a built-in benefit of teamwork, which sets it apart from individual action. An individual acting alone may be praised, blamed, or ignored; a team that does its work will be praised not only for its work but for its *teamwork*. In joining a team, you qualify for double kudos: the kudos for doing what you do and the kudos for doing it together, as a unit.

Teams promise not only to satisfy personal needs but to meet the exigencies of the age. "Teamwork is needed today as never before," people say, or "The twenty-first-century classroom must emphasize teamwork." Proponents of this idea cite the fluidity of workplaces and markets, the need for collaboration with others around the world, and the need for efficient systems of collaboration. Somehow, this became equated with teamwork. This equation should be scrutinized.

Indeed, some fields can benefit from teams—especially where the work requires multiple kinds of expertise. The statistician Andrew Gelman points out that in the social sciences, few people have all the requisite knowledge and skills for every aspect of research, from data-gathering to publicity, so it makes sense to divide the labor.[6] Yet such division of labor could destroy the integrity of a work of literary criticism or history; certain fields and projects require individual voice and mind. Thus, when deciding whether to use a team structure, one should consider the nature of the project at hand. No matter what century we live in, we require a range of work, thought, and relationships; no single trend should dictate the course of life. If it does, it will impoverish the whole.

The team (in theory and practice) has at least as many drawbacks as advantages. Each advantage comes with a pitfall. Teams need not be abolished altogether, but they require scrutiny and pruning.

First, just as teams focus on accomplishing concrete goals, so concrete goals may limit teams' possibilities. For example, a team tasked with writing a curriculum may make quick decisions about its contents and then write it up according to district guidelines—listing the standards that will be addressed; explaining how each unit and lesson will meet the standards; providing details on assessments, materials, and projects; and so forth. But a good curriculum requires grounding in the subject matter itself; to write it, one must think about the subject, consider various ways of shaping and presenting it, and find ways to build students' knowledge and foster their thinking. Curriculum writing is a concrete task, but it involves study, questioning, and introspection, activities that a team may "deprioritize," to put it mildly.

Teams not only focus on concrete goals but respond quickly to external demands. Describing how the contemporary market requires continual learning and adaptation, Harvard Business School professor Amy C. Edmonson points to the need for "teaming"—that is, continually working on temporary teams, which realign and regroup as necessary. According to Edmonson, even a symphony is a team, in that each member plays a specific part in a coordinated whole. "The players understand that they succeed or fail together," she writes; "they win or lose as a team." Similarly, she says, "corporations and organizations also win or lose by creating wholes that are greater than the sum of their parts."[7]

While Edmonson's vision of teams seems to make room for initiative and reflection—indeed, she writes of "leadership with a small 'l'"—her continual call for teaming presents its own problems. Such responsiveness to the market runs the risk of subservience; there is little room for stepping back from the market, resisting the external pressure for change, and thinking clearly about what one is doing. In a "teaming" environment, much energy goes into adaptation; one may not even have the needed perspective to question what is going on.

In offering respite from self, a team may lure its members into unwitting selfishness. The altruism of teamwork can be illusory. For instance, the team may engage in unethical competition, without the team members' knowledge; thus, thinking that they are helping others and contributing to a larger cause, the team members may actually conspire to knock others down. In the name of the "team," a company may even pit employees against each other, demanding, as in the case of the highly successful car service Uber, "super-pumpedness" from everyone.[8] Also, the very nature of the work may harm others—for instance, if the team produces a search engine that compromises users' privacy. The team members may not even consider how their work affects others; their focus will be on the product's immediate success. Granted, market selfishness exists with or without teams—but teams can blind themselves to their work by reveling in the virtues of the team itself.

Everyday scenarios illustrate the potential selfishness of teams. Some-times, at the grocery store, a couple will work together at the front of the line, while the cashier is scanning their items. One of them will go back to the shelves for more groceries, while the other holds their place. They might even discuss what kind of milk to get or which tomatoes would be better for the stew—all of this while the cashier is tallying up the total and others are waiting behind them. The teamwork is impeccable and suc-cessful; the couple deftly combines two tasks in one. Yet in doing this, they show disregard for the others and break the basic rules of queuing.

A team can disparage and suppress individuals who stand out. Teams require ease of action. Those who obstruct it, question it, or even slow it down may be treated like a splinter: ejected through immune reaction and pressure. Ostracism by teams (in the name of the team) has been well documented; the scholar David Seibold and his colleagues describe this as "the dark side of teams." A study by researchers at the University of Ottawa suggests that ostracism is both more common and more harmful in workplaces than overt harassment.[9]

In an interview with *Harvard Business Review*, J. Richard Hackman, professor of social and organizational psychology at Harvard, explained how teams do not live up to their hype.[10] In particular, he said, teams can be intolerant of the "deviant," the one who brings up uncomfortable, risky ideas:

> [The] deviant veers from the norm at great personal cost. Deviants are the individuals who are willing to say the thing that nobody else is willing to articulate. The deviant raises people's level of anxiety, which is a brave thing to do. When the boat is floating with the current, it really is extraordinarily courageous for somebody to stand up and say, "We've got to pause and probably change direction." Nobody on the team wants to hear that, which is precisely why many team leaders crack down on deviants and try to get them to stop asking difficult questions, maybe even knock them off the team. And yet it's when you lose the deviant that the team can become mediocre.

If, as Hackman suggests, the team resists serious questioning, it will choose not only the safer route but the safer people, the ones who stay firmly within the norm. Granted, a team *could* make room for unpopular ideas, but only by breaking with its team identity. Dissent appears uncooperative, even grumpy; in the name of cooperation, unity, and positivity, the team goes along with itself.

A team's cheerleader spirit can annoy as much as it inspires. Slogans like "Alone we can do so little; together we can do so much" (quoted from one of Helen Keller's speeches) means little out of context and strains the patience when overused.[11] Its truth depends on context; in some situations, an individual can do more than a group, while in others, the group can do more. "There's no 'I' in 'team'" can be similarly off-putting; is it good to get rid of the "I"? And what to make of the lack of "I" in "alone"? Team jargon quickly becomes not only overbearing but preposterous.

Along similar lines, the team's illusion of hipness, of being in step with the times, ignores those who stand somewhat outside of the times: those who view trends from a distance and do not try to be always up to date. These people focus on other things: work, friendships and families, or independent projects and pursuits. Though "out of it" in relation to team culture, they may be breaking ground in private. The team that prides itself on being cutting-edge may have no knowledge of edges.

Infatuated with the idea of the twenty-first-century team, workplaces and other institutions have begun heralding it as a matter of course. This obligatory obeisance gets in the way of initiative, flexibility, and cooperation—supposedly attributes of the twenty-first century. There is no reason for the team to lord it over the others; in fact, that seems quite unteamly. In the spirit of "team spirit," the team could allow for something other than the team.

Some will say that teams can be strong or weak, good or bad, and that the problems, when they occur, come from *poor organization* of teams, not from teams themselves. If that were so, then people would not say, with such pride, "There's no 'I' in 'team.'" They seem strangely cheery about the phrase's hyper-collectivism, which would give some people hives. If there is no "I" in "team," the least the team can do is admit to its limitations. Other kinds of association deserve recognition.

What other kinds of association exist?

There is the ensemble: more specifically, the orchestra, chorus, chamber group, or theater company. Let us consider the orchestra and theater company in particular. The orchestra seems like a team in many ways; each member plays a strictly delineated part, and all the parts come together into a whole. While there may be soloists, the general work is collective. In addition, the orchestra works together to prepare and perform pieces. How, then, is it not a team?

For an orchestra, the mastery of the piece is the starting point, not the end goal. The members learn their parts independently and come to rehearsal prepared. Except in amateur orchestras, or with especially tricky pieces, they do not devote rehearsal to basic technique. Instead, they shape the piece according to the conductor's and soloists' interpretations. The piece attains not only precision but an individual soul; while made of a group, the music transcends the group. It plays out the imagination of composer, soloist, and conductor; it offers the audience a way of hearing the piece, different from other ways. Thus, while the orchestra may start out somewhat like a team, it ends up as something else.

Some might argue that the orchestra works not only to perform a piece but to achieve a successful result—for instance, applause from the audience. This is only partly true. While any orchestra hopes for enthusiastic applause, it cannot treat this as a primary goal. Applause can vary according to the mood of the audience on a given night. If an orchestra were to aim for standing ovations, the entire endeavor would be distorted. There might be an announcement at the beginning: "Please remember to stand up at the end to show your appreciation. That's how we know you care." Then standing ovations would become habitual and lose their meaning. An orchestra cannot aim primarily for concrete external results without losing something.

It seems fitting, therefore, to call an orchestra something other than a team. The word "orchestra" will do just fine; otherwise "ensemble" has the right spirit. Something similar can be said for a theater company. There, too, the actors are working together to create a performance; their endeavor cannot be reduced to measurable goals, even though such goals figure in the whole. A play, moreover, is filled with solos; typically each character has a distinct story, desire, and voice. In acting there is continual interplay between solitude and relationship.

What about the faculty of an educational institution? In K–12 education, it has become common to refer to subject-matter departments as "teams": the English team, the math team, and so forth. This has even made its way into colleges. While the work of an English department involves something like teamwork, it cannot be reduced to that; there is no intellectual work without independence of thought. For example, one teacher's understanding of *Hamlet* may exceed that of his colleagues. Instead of seeking a "team" strategy for teaching *Hamlet*, perhaps this teacher could take the lead—by holding faculty seminars or giving a lecture on the work. The teachers could coordinate some of their work but otherwise allow for individual autonomy and strength. The word "faculty" (in the European sense—i.e., an academic division) may convey the appropriate commonality and autonomy.

So far I have discussed the ensemble and faculty. What is an appropriate term for people who come together to pursue or discuss a shared interest—say, in literature? Here "team" is clearly off the mark; "association," denoting a loose grouping of individuals with a common interest, may serve the purpose. An association may hold a conference, put out a publication, or even pursue political action—but generally the members are free to express their views and conduct their own lives. Often membership carries no obligations beyond payment of a fee. One joins not to be part of a fast-paced work unit but to associate with others (hence the term "association"), receive news, contribute voluntarily to projects, and take part in events.

Then there are forms of close collaboration—for instance, between editor and writer, coach and player, or teacher and student. These, like most of the other groups discussed here, have some characteristics of teams but are not exactly teams. They might be called partnerships or mentorships instead. Sometimes more than one word is needed. "Partnership" applies better to the editor-writer pair than to mentor-student pairs. The editor and writer are roughly equals; the writer originates the work, while the editor helps bring it to its final form. Mentorships and teacher-student relationships, in contrast, have a built-in inequality: one teaches or guides the other, for the sake of the other. The student or mentee is there to learn and improve; he or she has no emotional obligation to the guide but can (in the best of circumstances) acknowledge what he or she has given. This unequal yet dignified relationship requires a special name; "mentorship" serves the purpose, although it may need further qualification.

Finally we come to friendship, the relationship with the most freedom and individuality. Here two or more people come together out of affinity and mutual regard. Contingent, temporal friendships may exist for some kind of utility, be it entertainment, connections, or emotional support. Even these limited friendships enjoy freedom; the two come together and separate as they wish. They may work as teams temporarily, for specific purposes ("You chop the onions, and I'll get the broth going"), but goals and concrete roles do not define them. Friendships hint at the infinite; we lack the energy or compassion to be friends with everyone, but those few friends can open our understanding. The word "friend" has been trivialized but has not lost its meaning entirely; rather, it has called for various qualifiers: "online friend," "friend-slash-acquaintance," "childhood friend," "good friend," and other terms. No matter what forces pull away at friendship, it stands strong in its capacity for good.

The list could go on (to guild, club, congregation, assembly, forum, and more), but this is a promising start. Some might ask: Why bother with all those words? What's wrong with using "team" widely and recognizing its variations? The simple answer is that they are not all teams and that it is deceptive to refer to them as such. There are still more reasons.

Life has times of sharp loneliness. At some point, most of us feel out of sorts with our surroundings: maybe we don't fit in at work, or we have no good friends in the area. Recognizing different kinds of associations, and having different words for them, we can perceive the possibilities. I may have no close friends nearby right now, but I can be an audience member this evening. I may not qualify to join an acting company or actors' guild, but I can take a class. Even within a workplace, where the team typically rules supreme, I can recognize different ways of being with others. Some colleagues may become friends; others, acquaintances. One faculty meeting may resemble a public forum; another, a work session. The variety gives hope; somewhere, in these many configurations, I can find a place.

Many groups and associations need the perspective and protest of outsiders. Not all hands and minds are meant to contribute to a common goal; some work and speak through difference, through an urgent sense of wrongness in the world. This does not mean that they lack all association; rather, their associations take different forms. Some belong to dissident organizations; others revel in friendship. Some present papers at conferences; others play songs at concerts. Through not fitting in, they find their place among others.

Keeping in mind that not everything has to be a team, workers and leaders can configure relationships according to the project at hand. Some projects may require individual forays; others, sustained partnerships. Some may benefit from plenary discussion; others, from tightly coordinated efforts. Loosening the team's grip, and seeking the proper forms, will make workplaces wiser and quicker at once.

Finally, a good reason to break up the "team" concept is that it has gone too far. Like a wayward despot, it needs reining in. A rich vocabulary can function as a citizenry; when a given word oversteps its powers, other words can speak up. Finally, through checks and balances, words find their way to good uses.

Teams themselves will be better off if they cede some terrain. Just as a person can gain strength and focus from limitations, so can the team. Why should it feed on the world's increase, unless it offers something too? The best gift it can offer is modesty. Then it can do its work; people will join and leave it, but it will continue to offer its particular goods. In not pretending to be everything, it will live by a worthy principle. Let the team take its place alongside friendships, guilds, forums, ensembles, and solitudes. A choice of words can open up a life.

# 4

# IS LISTENING PASSIVE?

In 1992, a pianist couple started giving concerts in a worn-down community center, formerly a renowned concert hall, in Morristown, New Jersey. He would perform solo, she with her ensemble. When playing, they were struck by the quality of the acoustics. If only they could refurbish the building, they thought, it would draw musicians and audiences from around the world. They called upon their friend, a conductor in Russia, who flew right over, came inside, and gazed at the walls teeming with mud, icicles, and fungi. He clapped his hands, snapped his fingers, listened to the sounds, and declared that the Kirov Orchestra would perform there. In 1994, the refurbished Community Theatre started a new and magnificent life; in 2000, it became the subject of a book. Now named the Mayo Performing Arts Center, it has featured artists from the Kirov Orchestra to Ringo Starr to Diana Ross. [1]

It was no coincidence that the two pianists and conductor heard something in the air. The husband, Ukrainian-born Alexander Slobodyanik, one of the finest pianists of his time, had played concerts around the world for years before settling in Morristown with his American-born wife and colleague, Laryssa Krupa. Their visitor, Valery Gergiev, was at this point conductor of the Kirov and had already begun conducting internationally. It was their exceptional listening that transformed this community center; someone else might have looked at the building and seen real estate potential. The building might have been torn down and turned into a Party City store.

Listening can transform us and our surroundings, but today it gets little honor. People value quick interaction, not sustained attention to words and sounds. Of course there are exceptions, particularly among musicians—but in everyday life and in schools, listening takes a backseat to noisy activities that supposedly promote engagement.

Yet ancient traditions treat listening as the highest mental and spiritual activity. In his essay "On Listening to Lectures" ("De auditu," in *Moralia*), the Greek philosopher Plutarch (ca. 46–120 CE) points to the great responsibility of the listener. Some people, he observes, believe that only the speaker has a duty to fulfill—that the listeners just sit back and do what they please. "They think it only right," he writes, "that the speaker shall come with his discourse carefully thought out and prepared, while they, without consideration or thought of their obligations, rush in and take their seats exactly as though they had come to dinner, to have a good time while others toil." Plutarch takes these idlers to task, calling the listener "a participant in the discourse and a fellow-worker with the speaker." Not only does the listener contribute silently to the discourse, but he must work diligently, over many years, to listen well. He must cultivate a kindly yet critical spirit, avoiding the extremes of contempt and enthusiasm. [2]

Excellence of listening, according to Plutarch, requires not only self-discipline but introspection; just as a person about to leave a barbershop inspects his hair carefully to assess the difference between then and now, "so on his way home from a lecture or an academic exercise, it would be a shame not to direct his gaze forthwith upon himself and to note carefully his own spirit, whether it has put from it any of its encumbrances and superfluities, and has become lighter and more cheerful." A good lecture, according to Plutarch, has a purifying effect; it brings forth not murky and confused emotions but clarity. Whoever listens with alert and inquisitive spirit comes closer to wisdom. [3]

Plutarch's words seem far from us today. In his 2012 article "Twilight of the Lecture" (*Harvard Magazine*), Craig Lambert describes the epiphany of physicist Eric Mazur, who realized that his students had learned almost nothing after a semester of physics. So he tried something different: instead of explaining concepts himself, he had the students explain them to each other. This worked so well that he replaced his lectures with interactive learning. His findings took the world by storm. Lambert explains excitedly that "interactive pedagogy . . . turns passive, note-taking students into active, de facto teachers who explain their ideas to each other and contend for their points of view."[4] Unlike Plutarch, Lambert and Mazur set up an opposition between supposedly passive listening and active learning. They do not consider the intense activity of extended listening; with a curious passivity, they dismiss such listening offhand.

In dismissing sustained listening, they perpetuate part of the problem. Listening not only demands intense mental activity but takes years of practice. It is not easy to accomplish: the mind wanders; the body presses in with its hunger, fatigue, and unrest. If this happens during a concert or play, you may miss the best part or a part that makes sense of all the rest. If it happens during a lecture, you may lose a key connecting point in the argument. It takes discipline to pay attention to something from start to finish—and that is only the beginning. You must also assemble the details in the mind, make sense of the whole, and possibly formulate questions.

Students should not have to listen to lectures, and only lectures, throughout an entire course; even lecture courses are supplemented with discussions and labs. But if teachers abandon lectures altogether, how will students learn to take in the many parts of a presentation or performance and assemble them into a whole? If we lose the capacity to take in an extended presentation, our own expression and study will likewise be compromised. We will start thinking and writing in short bits and will not even have the patience for something more involved and complex. Twitter will become the dominant mode of conversation; the half-sentence will rule discourse and reason. Our presidents will tweet before thinking.

What is involved in listening? Setting aside the physiological processes, let us consider the mental activity involved. *Oxford English Dictionary* offers a definition of the verb "to listen": "to give attention with the ear to some sound or utterance; to make an effort to hear something; to 'give ear.'"[5] Listening is thus active by definition; it involves paying deliberate attention. Roland Barthes and Richard Havas posit three kinds of listening: (1) the orientation of the hearing to certain alerts or indices, (2) the act of deciphering, and (3) the act of entering into a relation with another, "an interlocution in which the listener's silence will be as active as the locutor's speech."[6] Listening, according to Barthes and Havas, involves not only detecting signals, not only making sense of sounds, but devoting attention to others and thus giving of oneself. It is a mutual act; the listener and the speaker give each other their attention and thoughts.

To illustrate the intricacies of listening, I will describe cantillation, the ritual chanting of Hebrew text, which has an intricate system of melodic phrases known as *te'amim* or *trop*. I choose this example because it is inherently interesting and because it illuminates the relationship between listening and reading. My discussion draws on Joshua Jacobson's landmark book *Chanting the Hebrew Bible*, as well as principles and details that I learned in Cantor Perry Fine's cantillation class at the Jewish Theological Seminary in 2016–2017.[7] The analysis and interpretation of Numbers 35:5 is my own, except where otherwise noted.

In Jewish ritual and study, there is no absolute division between listening and argument; the two work closely together. The root of the Hebrew word "shema"—the first word of the Shema prayer, essential and central to Judaism—means not only "to hear" but to hear fully and live accordingly.[8] To understand something, one must take it into the mind, turn it this way and that, question it, and make sense of it. Arguably, one must get into an argument with it.

Argument inheres in the reading and discussion of Torah. At many synagogues, each bar or bat mitzvah[9] gives a *dvar Torah*, a teaching on the Torah portion of the day, in which he or she poses a question about the text, cites contrasting responses to the question (from the Talmud and other sources), and offers a theory or answer, thereby entering the dialogue of many centuries. To enter Jewish life is to enter contemplative debate.

Listening and argument are intertwined. One cannot comment on a text unless one has listened to it. Listening takes many forms, but there is something special about doing so in the presence of the reader. Under Jewish law, it is a communal obligation to hear the Torah read aloud—from a scroll, with precise pronunciation and phrasing. This obligation is not fulfilled unless at least ten people (a *minyan*) hear it with understanding. The melody assists with this.

Centuries ago, Judaism developed an intricate system of cantillation—that is, of reading the text melodically—to aid the understanding, bring out the text's beauty, communicate with God, and separate the sacred from the profane. The oldest surviving Hebrew Bible with cantillation marks (as we know them today) is the Aleppo Codex of the tenth century—but Talmudic commentaries point to an older tradition. The scholar Lewis Glinert names five parameters of cantillation: absolute key, volume, tempo, rhythm, and spacing, which, when executed correctly, result in "a congregation leaning forward in its seats, and joining in what is essentially a group experience to which anyone can actively contribute, fulfilled in the bosom of the minyan."[10]

The melodic phrases of cantillation, known as "trop" or sometimes "trope," are indicated by symbols, te'amim, which appear to have originated in chironomy (hand signals). The system of cantillation has stable underlying principles. Each symbol represents not only a melodic phrase but a relation to other melodic phrases. The te'amim are divided into "kings" and "servants" and arranged in a hierarchy. The "kings" are disjunctive te'amim; that is, they do not lead directly into another phrase. The "servants," the conjunctive te'amim, must lead into something else; they cannot end a phrase or verse. Thus the symbols—and the melodic phrases they represent—provide clues to both grammar and meaning.

There are four levels of "kings" and "servants." At the highest level, level 1, of the hierarchy, there is the siluk, which looks like a large colon and indicates the end of a verse. At the same level, the etnachta, a caret-like mark below the appropriate stressed syllable, signals the "semicolon," or the place where the verse divides in two. (In the Hebrew Bible, most verses divide in this manner.) The two "halves" of the verse need not be close in length, yet they balance semantically. One can often find parallels and symmetries between the two parts of a verse; through examining them, one can come to understand the verse in new ways.

Each of the subsequent three levels has its own disjunctive te'amim. The melodic phrases often come in familiar sequences that an experienced reader can anticipate. While the specific melodies vary from place to place, shul to shul (synagogue to synagogue), and reader to reader, the structure and principles remain constant.

There are six melodic systems: for Torah, Haftarah, High Holiday Morning Service, Esther, Festive Megillot (Song of Songs, Ruth, and Ecclesiastes), and Lamentations; all use the same principles of cantillation, but they vary in their specific procedures. The Torah reader must read from a scroll without vowel or cantillation marks. To prepare a portion, he or she must learn the precise pronunciation, phrasing, and trop—preferably without fully memorizing the portion, since it should be read from the scroll, not recited from memory. This near-memorization is essential to the ultimate reading. Even master readers will make mistakes or stumble if they have not studied the portion in advance; those who memorize their portions may falter when one portion reminds them of another, or when they forget a word or phrase.

Thus it is not enough to learn the pronunciation and melody, especially if one reads regularly. To prepare well, one must come to know the portion's structure, meaning, and flow. Some people analyze the trop structure and ponder parts of the text, looking up words not only for their immediate definitions, but for their etymology, nuances, and history. Preparation becomes a form of textual study, a way of listening to the text. This is where argument comes in; when studying, one ends up asking: Why is this trop here? or Why is the word pronounced in this way? Through investigating these questions, one may come to the essence of the text.

It was cantillation—specifically, a recording of the Blessing before Haftarah—that drew me into my Judaism in the first place. A few months before my forty-ninth birthday, I came upon a recording of the Blessing Before Haftarah and began playing it over and over and learning the melody and words, my first Hebrew words. The Haftarah is chanted after the Torah at services. Each Haftarah selection comes from one of the books of the Prophets (for instance, Isaiah, Ezekiel, or Jeremiah). There is a blessing before and after the chanted text. The Blessing Before Haftarah is chanted in Haftarah mode—that is, it has the same scale and melodic phrases as the Haftarah readings themselves. Thus, without realizing it, I was learning my first trop.

The sound rafted me in. I listened and listened, then practiced the blessing over and over until I remembered it. I took the text everywhere with me and continued learning. During my hours of study, the sun changed its angles; I heard the words in gold, green, and blue. Little did I know where this would lead. A year and three months later, I chanted my first Haftarah in synagogue; soon after that, I started reading Torah. Cantillation became a beloved and luminous part of my life.

What is cantillation to those who practice and hear it? Focusing on a single verse of Torah—Numbers 35:5—I will speak first of the reader (the one who delivers the cantillation) and then of the listener.

In the passage leading up to Numbers 35:5, God tells Moses what instructions to give the people regarding distribution of land to the Levites, who because of their priestly status may not own land but may live on it and cultivate it. The verse in question deals with the measurements. In English translation, it seems straightforward, even dull: "You shall measure off two thousand cubits outside the town on the east side, two thousand on the south side, two thousand on the west side, and two thousand on the north side, with the town in the center. That shall be the pasture for their towns."[11]

In the Hebrew text, two phrases repeat four times: *et peat* ("the side") and *al'payim ba'amma* ("two thousand cubits"). The melody changes with each turn of direction (east, south, west, and north), transforming the seeming sameness into a kaleidoscope of sound.

Figure 4.1 shows, first, the Hebrew text with vowel and cantillation marks and then, below, an approximation of the melody and transliteration.[12] Each iteration of *et peat* or *ve-et peat* through *baamma* has a different melody (and occurs on a different line of the musical score). The four melodies progress from complex to simple as they approach the *etnachta*, the melodic phrase (at *batavekh*) that divides the verse in two parts. This melodic variety is due to the "stepping segments" in the verse; according to the syntactic rules, the individual measurements are not equal within the hierarchy of the verse but instead occupy a nesting structure. Each member of the list "nests" the previous one; thus the first iteration is nested within the second, the second within the third, and the third within the fourth, so that at the end, the list constitutes a unity.[13] Someone well versed in cantillation would hear not only melodic variety but accumulation and building. (A recording of this verse is available on my website.[14])

The four phrases of measurement ("et peat . . . alpayim baamma") occur in the second through fifth lines of the musical score of figure 4.1. Below the musical notes, there is a transliteration of the Hebrew; above the notes, the symbol and name of the final disjunctive melodies of each of the four phrases of measurement and the *etnachta*. (I have left out other *te'amim* and names for the sake of simplicity.) The first phrase, *et peat kedma alpayim baamma* ("on the east side, two thousand cubits"), ends in a level 4 disjunctive, *karnei farah*, or "bull's horns." (This is the sole occurrence of *karnei farah* in the entire Torah.) The next phrase, *ve-et peat negev alpayim baamma* ("on the south side, two thousand cubits"), ends in a level 3 disjuntive, *azla*. The next, *ve-et peat yam alpayim baamma* ("on the west side, two thousand cubits"), ends in a *revia*, a level 3 disjunctive (which nests the previous level 3 within it); and the last, *ve-et peat tzafon alpayim baamma*, in a *tippecha*, a level 2 disjunctive, which

וּמַדֹּתֶ֨ם מִח֤וּץ לָעִיר֙ אֶת־פְּאַת־קֵ֨דְמָה אַלְפַּ֜יִם בָּֽאַמָּ֗ה וְאֶת־פְּאַת־נֶ֜גֶב
אַלְפַּ֣יִם בָּאַמָּ֗ה וְאֶת־פְּאַת־יָ֞ם ׀ אַלְפַּ֣יִם בָּאַמָּ֗ה וְאֵ֨ת פְּאַ֥ת צָפ֛וֹן אַלְפַּ֥יִם
בָּאַמָּ֖ה וְהָעִ֣יר בַּתָּ֑וֶךְ זֶ֚ה יִהְיֶ֣ה לָהֶ֔ם מִגְרְשֵׁ֖י הֶעָרִֽים

(Numbers 35:5)

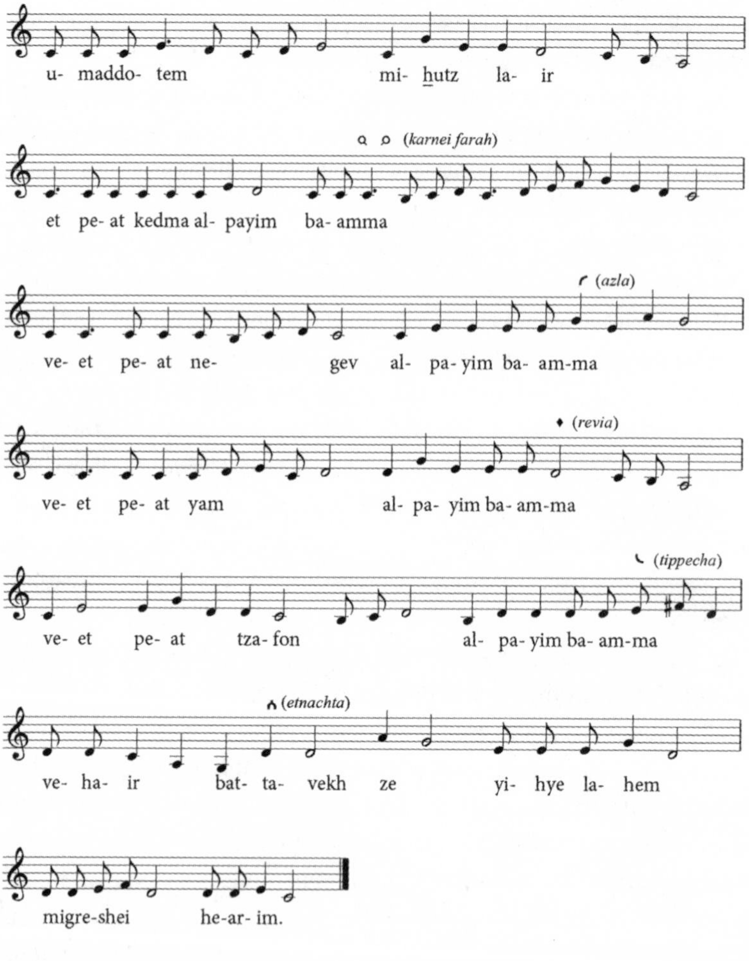


**Figure 4.1. Text and Cantillation Melody of Numbers 35:5 (Hebrew Bible).** ***Sheet music prepared by Diana Senechal. Hebrew text and melody in public domain.***

leads into the level 1 *etnachta* (at "batavekh"). In each case, the disjunctive in question occurs on the last syllable of *baamma*.

Why such colorful melody, why such intricate progression, in this seemingly ordinary verse? The syntax and grammar alone explain it, but through syntax and grammar, one can find meaning. Some commentators perceive a warning regarding routine duties: they may seem exciting at first, but if we do not take heed, they gradually become rote. Just as the melodies here progress from the unique to the common, so our rituals might become dull and stale if we do not pay attention to them. [15] Or the reverse interpretation might hold: even the most mundane tasks contain beauty and meaning; within repetition one can find great variety. Measuring two thousand cubits to the north is not the same as measuring two thousand to the east; the terrain and vistas vary, and the impressions accumulate. In addition, the verse brings out what can come of attentive reading and listening: how a seemingly ordinary sequence of words contains vistas and hidden places.

This verse is just a fraction of the Torah portion, which in turn is a fraction of the Torah—but one could listen to it hundreds of times and hear more in it. Listening has to do with hearing and putting together those patterns and details, finding meaning in them, and relating them to something larger. What one does with cantillation and Torah, one can do (in different ways) with listening in other contexts, including lectures.

I have focused on the chanter here, but cantillation is ultimately for the listeners; it conveys the text in clarity and beauty. No matter what one's level of Hebrew, one can gain something from listening. Some people hear the sounds but do not understand them; they read the English translation and sense a different dimension in the Hebrew sounds. Some can follow along but without understanding the Hebrew; they might look back and forth between the Hebrew and the translation. Some understand enough Hebrew to read along; still others understand cantillation and recognize moments like this, when a rare or unique *trop* appears. For some, these passages come with memories—of bar mitzvah readings, holidays, and more. Still others may have thought about a particular passage for years. Listening ascends to higher and higher levels; it is never complete. If sacred text (across religions) has something to offer to the secular world, it is the understanding that one can listen infinitely.

Let us return to the classroom lecture and then proceed to other kinds of listening. The lecture is not the only viable lesson format, but it contributes something indispensable to learning. In particular, it demands attention—on the part of both teacher and student—to structure and details. Through learning to perceive structure, students make sense of the material and form structures of their own.

Years ago, when I was taking an exam for a Russian-English bilingual teaching license, I was asked to describe, in English, one of my favorite teachers. This was supposed to be the easiest part of the test for me—it was in English, and no one really cared about the content of my response—but it proved the most difficult. Stumbling over my native tongue, I tried to describe John Hollander, with whom I studied poetry in college and graduate school. I remembered vividly what I had learned but could not sum it up. He took a poem and opened it up into music, architecture, other poems, other languages. Each class was a great romp; we rode along, trusting that he knew where we were going and that we too would learn the terrain. We read memorable poetry; we filled our ears with it. Hollander's lectures now remind me of cantillation; he would take up a poem and sound out the phrases, bringing out their origins, allusions, and contradictions.

I walked out of each class with a sense of clarity and amazement. I would go home and write—new poems, essays about poems, essays and stories about other things. I have taken many great courses in my life, but none surpassed the substance and liveliness of this one. The liveliness had nothing to do with how much I talked, though I did talk now and then. Rather, the lecture had a way of waking up my mind.

I am not presenting myself as an extraordinary listener; my listening is often poor. My mind wanders, not because I am bored but because something triggers a thought (as in Dante's *Purgatorio*, Canto 18, when he starts falling asleep: "I was so drawn from random thought / to thought that, wandering in mind, I shut / my eyes, transforming thought on thought to dream"[16]). My gifts or flaws are not the point here; what matters is the listening. Listening transforms sound; when you grasp the details and the whole, you have already turned it into something else. It has now become yours in a sense; it has entered your mind, not just in wisps and strands but as an entirety, even if you do not remember it all.

But listening is being pushed out the window. If "interactive learning" is now a college fad, it has long been mandated in K–12 education. It has some good, of course, but has been taken to absurd extremes. When the superintendents come by to visit classrooms, they want to see the students working in groups. Even the formal evaluation rubrics, such as the Danielson Framework, give higher ratings to lessons where students pose the questions and offer the answers.[17] If "teacher talk" absolutely must occur, the teacher is expected to keep it brief. The problem lies not in the idea of students talking but rather in the disparagement of extended speech by the teacher.

Granted, some of this hostility to extended listening has practical basis; teachers of K–12 education (and even college) find that students have short attention spans and will lose patience if they have to listen to anything for long. Books on classroom management advise teachers to do as little talking as possible.[18] But why not help students build up their listening? Listening is not an automatic skill; it is not something one "has" or "doesn't have." If schools do not help students build their listening, who will?

Before teaching others to listen, one must develop the capacity in oneself. Listening takes thousands of forms, yet any listening practice can strengthen one's overall patience, receptivity, and stamina. One can choose something to listen to regularly: musical recordings, poems, plays, speeches, and dialogues. Thousands of free recordings are now available on the Internet; the quality is often surprisingly good. Libraries have rare recordings—audiobooks, records, tapes, and other materials—that have not yet appeared online.

In addition, it is possible to listen to something in the mind. I have often done this: without humming or speaking, without even mumbling, I "play" a poem or piece of music in my mind from start to finish. I listen closely to the cadences and overtones. If it is music, I try to hear all the parts. At times it can approximate an actual performance without making a sound. In this way, one can hear a symphony in a library (without earphones).

I am not much of an advice-giver—but if I were to offer some tips on listening, this is what I would say.

Choose something to listen to, and be alone with it. Do nothing else while listening. Do not check e-mail, surf the web, read a book, or even exercise. The listening should be the only activity (in this case). Give it a time limit: either the length of the recording or a specific time interval such as half an hour.

Then listen away; take in the sounds, patterns, and meanings. Give as much as possible to the listening; do not cut it short or mix it with another task. If the mind wanders, bring it gently back. (Some mind-wandering is good; it could be the romp of the imagination.)

Keep on doing this day after day. Expand to different kinds of listening. Drill down and get more precise. Take instruction from the listening. Listen for sheer fun, too, without "making" anything of what you hear.

Play with the possibilities and find your own way of practicing. Take them out into the world; exercise this listening on the train, at meetings, in the classroom, in conversations with friends, and in the mind. You may find yourself looking forward to the practice. Not all listening is pleasant, of course, but there is beauty even in the unpleasant kinds. We cannot listen to everything, but we can listen well, beyond our immediate satisfactions.

Teachers strong in the practice of listening can help their students develop it. A student can tell when a teacher is listening—not only to the discussion, but to other things. A teacher can point out details and structure of a text and ask students for their own impressions. Someone in the room will notice something that everyone else missed, and students may ask, at that point, to listen again. Sometimes students will argue over what they heard—again calling for a repeat. Listening becomes a way into questioning.

School leaders, too, can create a culture of listening. If I were running a school, I would institute a full period of listening at the start of every day. The material would vary; students might listen to a poem, a musical composition, or a radio theater show. The "listening hour" (or forty-five minutes, most likely) would become a favorite part of the day—not only for its inherent rewards but for its lack of pressure. Students would not have to produce anything afterward: no writing, conversation, ratings, or anything else. The listening would be enough in itself.

Without listening, we grow lazy and crude; we bathe in ourselves and our certainties. We reject things that push, disturb, and shake us, even things that delight us. But the situation can be repaired at any moment; there is always something to listen to, even in the mind.

When my family lived in Moscow for a year, we had two little rooms and a kitchen. There was no living room; my sister and I shared one room and my parents the other. There was nowhere to go for privacy. Wherever I went in the apartment, there was at least one other person present. Then I discovered the rooms of music.

My parents had a stereo in their room; almost every day I would come in to listen to records. My collection was small, but I treasured everything in it (and remember, to this day, how each one sounded): Natalia Gutman and Sviatoslav Richter performing Schubert's Arpeggione Sonata; Emil Gilels performing Chopin's Piano Concert in E Minor; Gutman and Richter performing Beethoven's cello sonatas; and Alexander Slobodyanik performing Liszt's Piano Sonata in B Minor. We had no headphones, but when I put on a record and closed my eyes, I had all the room I needed, at least for the music. I came to know the tones of each note; I came to notice something new each time. Listening to Slobodyanik play Liszt— yes, the same Slobodyanik who, years later, helped renew the concert hall in Morristown—I learned how much temperament can hide in a single note, how many births and ruptures, how many turns.

I have listened to many renditions of Liszt's sonata, but I still love Slobodyanik's the most. I think of the hushed beginning, the bursts and silences, the unexpected chords, the internal logic and soul. When I returned to it recently, I realized that the apartment in Moscow had pushed me into listening, and listening into expanse. The listening was my opening and my home.

Listening is good; very well. Some counterarguments are in order, here, though, especially regarding listening in the classroom. First, it is impossible (and undesirable) to listen to everything. I don't want to spend an evening with mediocre music or sit through a tedious and vacuous speech. I don't like listening to vicious gossip or endless complaining. To listen to some things, one must be willing to shut out others. Yet this selective listening can become insular: a person takes in what already seems pleasant, interesting, or desirable and excludes everything else. How does one listen selectively while remaining open to challenges and surprises?

The lack of an easy answer suggests that listening cannot serve as a panacea. It takes years to cultivate the judgment and adventurousness essential to listening. Young children need help selecting what they will hear; they may like certain things instinctively but rely on adults for basic repertoire. (According to Plutarch, the Greek philosopher Xenocrates recommended putting ear-guards on children to protect them from vile words.[19]) As they grow into their teenage years and adulthood, they start testing their own judgment and choosing their material. A questioning attitude will help at every stage.

Some will ask whether students shouldn't be held *accountable* for their listening. Shouldn't they have to write something afterward, to show that they were really paying attention? Yes, at times teachers should require students to write about something they just listened to. This will help both student and teacher ascertain what was learned and what was not. But there should also be listening with no additional requirements. This simplicity allows for liberty and focus; instead of having to produce something, students may simply think, ruminate, and remember.

Perhaps the strangest aspect of listening is the mutuality, even when the speaker or musician is not present. The performer has the sense of being heard; to speak, sing, or play, even from memory, is to exercise imagination, as the listener could be someone far away, in a different era or country. To perform is to be astonished. The listener, too, meets the performer with astonishment; although the recording may have been made decades ago, it plays now, and the gap of ages does not matter.

Through listening together and alone, we measure our cubits; we discover vistas in a humdrum task; we find questions gleaming in the corners of arguments; we descend the long slopes of words; we search, find, lose, and search again; we find each other; we turn a concert hall into its own magnificence.

# 5

# RESEARCH HAS SHOWN—JUST WHAT, EXACTLY?

Early in my teaching career, I attended many training sessions for teachers of English language learners. At one of these, we were given a quiz that included the question, "How long does it take an English language learner between 8 and 11 years old to master academic English?" The options were: (a) at least 0–2 years; (b) at least 2–4 years; and (c) at least 5–7 years. I thought (a) was possibly correct but selected (b) to be safe. The session leader revealed (c) as the correct answer: a student needed 5–7 years to master academic English. I squirmed, formed my words, and raised my hand.

"This can't be correct," I protested. I thought of classmates visiting from other countries who jumped into class discussion right away. I thought of my own experience in the Netherlands and the Soviet Union, where, within a year, I was participating fully in most of my classes. "There must be other factors—"

"Research has shown," the session leader said.

"But how can it be if—"

"Research has shown."

Before that day, I had thought of research as investigation of uncertainties; now it seemed to put an end to all questions. If research showed something, well, there was nothing you could say; you had to go along with it. "Research has shown"—the phrase struck me with its vagueness, its exaltation of research (regardless of quality), and its use as a mallet to quash discussion.

The research in question (by Virginia P. Collier and Wayne P. Thomas) reveals a more complex picture. Collier and Thomas found that, on the whole, economically advantaged students who arrived in the United States at ages eight to eleven needed five to seven years to reach the 50th percentile in standardized tests in *all* subjects—but within this general figure, there was variation, not only between but within subjects. Students exceeded the 50th percentile in mathematics within two years and reached the 50th percentile on the language arts standardized test (a low-level, skills-oriented test) within three. In contrast, they showed slower progress on reading tests. Other studies revealed similarly complex and subtle findings.[1] Moreover, these studies dealt with generalities and averages; I saw little discussion of outliers. Nor did I see much investigation of the nature of "academic" English and its relation to actual subject matter. The phrase "research has shown" was supposed to resolve everything but did not.

In this case, the research did not necessarily contradict my own experience. Visiting a country for a year carries different requirements from moving permanently. When you are in a country temporarily, you may not have to take the official tests; if you take part in classes, do the homework, and become functional (or better) in the language, you will exceed expectations. In contrast, if you move permanently to a new country, the stakes are higher; if you want a chance at college or employment, you must pass standardized tests (among other things). Even so, research does not "show" that it will take you at least five to seven years to do so; the exact time varies by individual and subject.

From here, I began noticing the phrase "research has shown" (and its relatives "science tells us" and "we now know") in contexts ranging from the classroom to the airplane. I found again and again that research did not "show" what people claimed it showed. Often the press oversimplified and exaggerated a study's conclusions; often the study's own abstract did the same. Often the study itself had obvious flaws or limited applications. Why, I asked, do people believe summaries of research so readily? Here I investigate the problem, show three typical examples, and propose a different relation to existing and future research.

"Research has shown"—the phrase offers both comfort and excitement. It suggests that we do not have to look into details; we can trust the "research," whatever it might be. It also carries a tone of authority: some expert, somewhere, has arrived at this (often incredible) finding, and our duty is not to question it, but to give it a dizzy ovation. "Research has shown" makes a packed auditorium swoon, but why? Where does this pale worship come from?

To question scientific research, one must, first of all, know what research is. It is not the last word, nor even the first; it poses a question, often an old or ongoing one, and investigates possible answers. It requires tight logic and wiggly skepticism; it flounders if it lurches headlong toward a desired conclusion. To do good research, one must test and doubt, test and doubt. Research should be taken for what it is; whether formal or informal, qualitative or quantitative, methodologically sound or flawed, exploratory or confirmatory, it should not have automatic status or authority but should instead undergo scrutiny. An aura surrounds the very mention of science, yet science, ironically, is no glowing herald but a way of working in continual uncertainty and fallibility. In the "research has shown" parade, tentative findings dress up as conclusions, impeding not only the scientific process but its questioning spirit.

I will give three examples of research popularized with false "research has shown" statements: the "lemon introvert test," the "ten thousand hours" theory, and the Implicit Association Test. In its popularized version—distinct from the research itself—each study plays into a pseudoscience of self: a belief that "science" can easily teach us things about ourselves and change the trajectory of our lives. Such pseudoscience depends on the belief that "research has shown" something clear, unambiguous, and immediately applicable.

Initially conducted by H. J. Eysenck and Sybil B. G. Eysenck in 1967, the lemon introvert test has been discussed and practiced far and wide.[2] According to the popular summaries, you can find out how introverted you are by testing how much saliva you produce in reaction to a drop of lemon juice on your tongue. All you need, according to the psychologist Brian Little, are a cotton swab, a thread, an eyedropper, concentrated lemon juice, and the tongue of a volunteer. Little writes:

> For some people the swab will remain horizontal. For others it will dip on the lemon juice end. Can you guess which? For the extraverts, the swab stays relatively horizontal, but for introverts it dips. . . . I have done this exercise on myself a number of times, and each time my swab dips deeply. I am, at least by this measure, a biogenic introvert.[3]

Assuming that Little has the Eysenck and Eysenck test in mind, his state-ment is incorrect; the original test in no way suggests that you can find out from your own salivation how introverted you are. It does not even suggest that introverts are more aroused by sensory stimuli than extro-verts. Yet these takeaways have run rampant; Susan Cain writes in her best seller *Quiet: The Power of Introverts in a World That Can't Stop Talking*:

> In one well-known experiment, dating all the way back to 1967 and still a favorite in psychology demonstration courses, Eysenck placed lemon juice on the tongues of introverts and extroverts to find out who salivated more. Sure enough, the introverts, being more aroused by sensory stimuli, were the ones with watery mouths.[4]

This is dubious at first glance; so many factors can lead to increased or decreased salivation that the statement should arouse immediate skepti-cism (especially in highly arousable introverts, if one follows Cain's line of reasoning). The actual study comes nowhere near showing what Little and Cain claim. Moreover, it does not reveal the raw data, so we do not know what happened behind the researchers' calculations.

Eysenck and Eysenck sought to demonstrate that extroversion was both unitary (a cohesive concept with correlating factors) and indepen-dent of other personality dimensions, such as neuroticism. They posited that if a criterion test could be found whose results correlated highly with extroversion, then one could determine whether extroversion was in fact unitary. By their logic, if extroversion was indeed unitary, then the test items "should have correlations with the criterion which were *proportion-al* to their factor loadings, and if the factor was independent of another factor, then the criterion should not correlate significantly with any test item constituting this other factor."[5] In other words (loosely), the more strongly a test item result correlates with extroversion overall, the more strongly it should correlate with the criterion test results; it should also not correlate with test items constituting another factor. For their criterion test, they chose a lemon juice test, in which four drops of lemon juice would be placed on the subject's tongue for twenty seconds, and the salivary reaction measured. If they could show a relation between extro-version test items and lemon test results—and no such relation for neuro-ticism test items—then they would be on their way to demonstrating the unitary nature of introversion.

Thus Eysenck and Eysenck were not analyzing individual responses to lemon juice; they focused instead on the relation, if any, between neuroticism and extroversion, through an analysis of correlation between lemon test results and test items. In this paper, they referred briefly to an earlier, unpublished lemon test study that suggested a correlation between increased salivation (in response to lemon juice) and introversion, stating that "extreme extroverts show little or no increment in salivation, while extreme introverts show an increment of almost 1 gram; intermediate groups show intermediate amounts of increment." They claimed to have found a correlation of 0.71 on fifty male and fifty female subjects between increment scores and introversion, with no difference between the sexes, but they gave no further details on the data or on the "intermediate amounts of increment." One can hypothesize that the middle range (between extroversion and introversion) showed indeterminate results—that only at the extremes could a clear correlation be found.

For the test at hand, Eysenck and Eysenck performed a lemon test on forty-five men and forty-eight women who also took a fifty-seven-question version of the Eysenck Personality Inventory (EPI). Here again, they measured the correlation between introversion and difference in salivation—but gave no more detail on this particular test than they gave on the earlier one. They stated simply that the lemon test had a loading of -0.74 on extroversion (that is, salivation increase correlated negatively with extroversion) and a loading of 0.01 on neuroticism. When they repeated the analysis on men and women separately, they found factor loadings of -0.70 and -0.60 on the extroversion factor and 0.02 and -0.06 on the neuroticism factor. In other words, they found a strong correlation between saliva increase and test responses suggestive of introversion—and no such correlation for neuroticism—but once again provided no details and no data.

From here, they correlated the factor loading (for introversion and neuroticism) of each individual test item on the EPI with the lemon test results: that is, they compared how results on test items indicative of extroversion and on test items indicative of neuroticism correlated with the lemon test results. They found, overall, a high correlation with extroversion and no significant correlation with neuroticism. This suggested to them that "factor-analytically," the lemon test seemed "a pure (univocal) measure of introversion"—that is, not a measure of neuroticism. Yet they recognized that "it might have been objected that such a comparison capitalizes on whatever non-relevant factors were present on the occasion of this experiment and might have influenced both the EPI responses of the *S*s and their lemon test scores."[6]

To address this potential problem, they next used factor loadings from another EPI test given on a separate occasion to five hundred subjects (men and women). This test had the same fifty-seven items plus fifty additional ones. They then plotted the factor loadings (for extroversion) of the original fifty-seven items (from this larger-scale test) against the items' correlation (in the previous test) with the lemon score. In other words, they plotted each test item's *correlation* with extroversion against its *correlation* with lemon test results.

Glancing at the graph, one might conclude that the more strongly a test item correlates with extroversion, the more strongly it also correlates with a lemon test result. But correlations between test items and the lemon never appear to reach 0.5 (a moderate correlation), and many are clustered between 0 and 0.3. In addition, many of the test items do not fit the pattern isolated by the researchers. Eysenck and Eysenck observe that "practically all the E items have high factor loadings on the extroversion factor and reasonable correlations with the lemon test, whereas N items have low loadings and low correlations." They use the lemon test to demonstrate the *independence* of extroversion from neuroticism. The correlations between the lemon test results and factor loadings for extroversion are "reasonable" but noisy and not especially strong. The studies in no way demonstrate that the more introverted you are, the more your saliva will increase in response to lemon juice.[7]

But newspapers and other media continue to propagate the lemon juice takeaway. In the *Science: Human Body and Mind* section of its website, the BBC reports that "the amount of saliva you produce after putting a drop of lemon juice on your tongue might tell you something about your personality." (Sure, but it also might not.) In *New York Magazine*, Melissa Dahl reports, with a pinch of skepticism, that "subsequent experiments have cast some doubt on this theory, as [Christian] Jarrett points out, but 'while it's still debatable whether the lemon test can accurately reveal your introversion, it certainly does tell you something interesting about your physical sensitivity.'" Plus, she notes, it can be done in the comfort of your home, "an introvert's favorite place to be." Well, yes, a lemon juice test can tell you whether you salivate in response to lemon juice—at least on this particular occasion.[8]

There is nothing wrong with performing lemon tests at home or salivating in private. But that's pure entertainment; the results say nothing definitive. While it may be true that extreme introverts and extreme extroverts have relatively high and low lemon test scores, respectively (and on average), we can expect a lot of variance. Research, in this case, has not linked our spit to our souls.

Let us now proceed to the second example of oversimplified and misapplied research. The "ten thousand hours" theory—coined by K. Anders Ericsson, popularized by Malcolm Gladwell in *Outliers*, and carried into other theories and concepts, such as Angela Duckworth's theory of "grit"—posits that to master a field, you need thousands of hours of practice. According to Gladwell, something important happens around the ten-thousand-hour mark. His version of the theory has since been widely debunked, and he has risen up to clarify himself. I will describe the original research and explain the problems with Gladwell's popularization—especially its catering to science as entertainment.

In "The Role of Deliberate Practice in the Acquisition of Expert Performance," Ericsson, Ralf Th. Krampe, and Clemens Tesch-Römer analyze expert performance to determine the relation between innate and acquired ability. The dichotomy between these two kinds of ability may not be present, they state, "when we examine the effects of over 10,000 hours of deliberate practice extended over more than a decade." They explain that "deliberate practice" involves more than plain repetition; one must engage in "careful monitoring and problem solving." They hypothesize, moreover, that "the amount of time an individual is engaged in deliberate practice is monotonically related to that individual's acquired performance." That is, once you are engaging in deliberate practice, you continue to improve with time.[9]

To investigate and develop their theory, they conducted two studies: one of the practice habits of violinists and another of expert and amateur pianists. Both studies focused on technical proficiency. In both cases, they found that the experts not only have more years and hours of practice but integrate their practice methodically and regularly into their schedules (which in turn suggests that they approach their practice deliberately, not haphazardly).

In the first study, they asked professors at the Music Academy of West Berlin to nominate violinists for two categories: the "best violinists," that is, those with a potential for careers as international soloists, and "good violinists." They then recruited a third group: "music teachers," or violinists in the music education program. Finally, they interviewed ten middle-aged violinists in symphony orchestras with international reputation. These subjects were interviewed in three sessions and asked to complete a taxonomy of practice activities followed by a daily log. [10]

All the violinists rated practice as the most relevant activity for improving violin performance. In addition, the "best" and "good" violinists (the ones nominated by music professors and the ones in orchestras) reported more frequent practice per week than the music teachers. The "best" and "good" young violinists differed not in the time spent practicing, but in their assessment and use of leisure time; the "good" violinists underestimated their leisure time (i.e., believed they had less than they had), whereas the "best" violinists did not. In addition, the "best" violinists spent more of their leisure time on music-related activities—so that, even when not practicing, they were building their musical knowledge. [11] There were many more findings (regarding sleep habits and other matters of lifestyle).

While this study suggested a strong association between practice and proficiency, it was limited to musicians who had already attained the latter. For the second study, the researchers compared the performance of expert and *amateur* pianists on a series of music tasks involving interpretation, precision, and replication. Here, too, they analyzed the subjects' practice, sleep, and other habits. For one task, the subjects were to work out a musical interpretation of the Prelude No. 1 in C Major by J. S. Bach and then try to reproduce it precisely when playing it three times. They were evaluated on both quality and consistency of performance. The researchers found that, regardless of skill level, those who had practiced more over their musical histories performed the task better. This applied to several parameters of technical performance and expressiveness. In addition, they found (both here and in the first study) that practice time for the best performers increased with age; that is, the older they were, the more they tended to practice. [12]

The researchers did not analyze what actually happens during practice; rather, they interpreted practice in the context of other activities. Practice was deliberate if the musicians knew how much time they spent at it and could accurately separate it from leisure. In addition, their schedule hinted at the quality of their practice; if they consistently practiced at their most productive time of day, and if they pursued music-related activities during their leisure time, this suggested an approach to practice that went beyond just putting in the hours. The researchers discovered, across the board, that musicians needed ten years of deliberate practice to attain mastery; this finding seemed to extend to other fields as well. [13]

I have not come close to describing the study in full—but even this summary reveals that Ericsson and his colleagues went beyond positing some magic number of practice hours. Their larger argument was that the best musicians made practice part of their life in a conscious, lucid, and rational way. Some questions remain unanswered: Could anyone—just anyone—become a top musician through deliberate practice, or does practice ability itself involve natural ability? In addition, as the researchers themselves ask, what role does motivation play? Do those who enjoy practicing at a young age find themselves practicing more, improving more, enjoying it even more, demanding more of themselves, and attaining greater proficiency? Also, must one always be analytical in one's practice, or is there value also in stepping away from analysis now and then? Why is it that some outstanding musicians go through periods of little or no practice—or begin playing during their teenage years? The picture remains complicated; there is no formula for musical success, but those at the top consistently show stronger practice habits (and more practice overall), according to the researchers, than those at lower levels.

Gladwell took the findings into his hands and rolled them into a glittering ball. Citing the examples of Bill Gates, Bill Joy, the Beatles, Mozart, and others, and referring to the Ericsson study, he wrote that "ten thousand hours is the magic number of greatness." He qualified this by saying that young people cannot possibly attain this number on their own initiative; they need intensive support from parents, schools, and other institutions. The "outliers," he pointed out, are all "beneficiaries of some kind of unusual opportunity"; they are not entirely self-made. All the same, according to Gladwell, something remarkable happens around that ten thousandth hour. Things start to click; the musicians, programmers, and others not only find their technique but hit upon their originality. [14] By emphasizing the ten thousand hours, he turned a serious finding into razzle-dazzle. Readers responded to the "wow" effect.

Gladwell set the tone for future work. Angela Duckworth's theory of "grit" combines the seriousness and sophistication of Ericsson with the popularizing flair of Gladwell; her work exhibits the tension between the two. Her idea was poised for fame; several years before her book appeared, her work was featured in Paul Tough's best seller *How Children Succeed: Grit, Curiosity, and the Hidden Power of Character.* Her TED talk, delivered in 2013, has been viewed nearly ten million times; in the same year, she was awarded a MacArthur Fellowship.[15]

Duckworth's theory—that high achievers differ from others not in intelligence but in "grit," or determination and direction—has some scientific basis but has suffered from zealous popularization and "research has shown" declarations. Grit does appear to correlate with long-term success in difficult endeavors. Yet despite uncertainties over its nature and over the possibility of teaching it, institutions and media have seized on it as the answer to education. Schools have devoted class time to measuring, cultivating, and even grading grit. Many administer the Grit Scale Test, which consists of twelve generic statements (e.g., "I have overcome setbacks to conquer an important challenge," "My interests change from year to year"), to which the test-taker responds in degrees of agreement or disagreement. Problems with such measurement abound; as Duckworth herself points out, responses can be affected by reference bias—that is, the test-taker's own standards and cultural expectations.[16]

Duckworth spoke out against such testing, calling it "a bad idea" and resigning from the board in control of the grit project in California.[17] A few months after her resignation, reports appeared about statistical inaccuracies in the book; to her credit, she admitted to the errors. The error of oversimplification, however, still needed to be addressed. Whatever the merits and drawbacks of Duckworth's research, it has been promoted as a "big idea"; in this capacity, it has led to a good deal of silliness.

The theories of ten thousand hours and grit—and their many variations and extensions—need less cheerleading and more investigation. To preserve the integrity of their work, the researchers can adopt subtler language, allow for complexity, stay grounded in academic and artistic disciplines, and continue to warn, as Duckworth has done, against excess and abuses. Grit must be for the sake of something, or it is just gravel.

I now move briefly to the third example of distorted research: the "Race IAT," or Implicit Association Test of racial preferences. In general, the IAT, developed by Mahzarin Banaji and Anthony G. Greenwald (who introduced it at a Seattle press conference in 1998), is designed to measure the strength of our mental associations. When taking the test, a subject must sort words and images into categories by hitting specific keyboard keys as quickly as possible. Valence IATs measure the positivity or negativity that we associate with a given concept; for instance, our results may suggest that we prefer women to men, young people to old people, or blacks to whites. It is this last test—of racial preference—that I discuss here.

In light of contemporary discussions of race, gender, and other questions of identity, what could be handier than a test that reveals your hidden biases? The IAT purports to do just that. By showing you images paired with words (for instance, white people paired with positive adjectives, black people paired with negative adjectives, and then a switching of the positive and negative associations) and timing your keyed responses, the test's authors claim to measure your hidden proclivities, such as your preference for one race over another. If, for instance, you take longer to pair a positive adjective with a black face than with a white face, this supposedly suggests that you prefer white people to black. Since the speed of your responses is out of your rational control, the IAT presumably measures preferences that you cannot consciously access but that are nonetheless real.

At this point it is unclear that it measures any such thing. In January 2017, nearly twenty years after the IAT had been introduced, Jesse Singal gave it a scathing exposé in *New York Magazine*. According to Singal, researchers and commentators have "offered it as a way to reveal to test-takers what amounts to a deep, dark secret about who they are: They may not feel racist, but in fact, the test shows that in a variety of intergroup settings, they will act racist." He quotes Gladwell, who waxes enthusiastic about the IAT in his best seller *Blink*: "The IAT is more than just an abstract measure of attitudes. It's a powerful predictor of how we act in certain kinds of spontaneous situations."[18]

Singal points out several weak or missing links in the researchers' arguments. First, evidence is mounting that the IAT does not meet the quality control standards for psychological instruments. Its test-retest reliability is questionable (people are likely to have different results from one sitting to the next); there is ongoing controversy over whether it predicts behavior; and previous research supporting the IAT's premises turns out to have numerous problems. Second, "the hype over IAT research, and the eagerness to apply the test to real-world problems, has so outpaced the evidence that it has launched a lot of studies built on underwhelming foundations." To examine how implicit bias affects society, Singal concludes, one needs "accurate tools"; a flimsy test does nothing to combat racism or any other social ill.[19]

Other journalists and reporters followed suit. In a *Vox* article in March 2017, German Lopez described his initial interest in the IAT and his subsequent doubts, inquiries, and conversations. He concluded that "the IAT may not amount to much" and that other means are required for combating racism. In December 2017, in a masterful takedown, Olivia Goldhill (*Quartz*) questioned the wisdom of measuring implicit bias in the first place. "The current hype around implicit bias, which overstates its role in both causing and combating discriminatory behavior, is both unwarranted and unhelpful," she writes. "Instead of looking to implicit bias to eradicate prejudice in society, we should consider it an interesting but flawed tool." Singal followed up two days later with another article, in which he called out the IAT researchers for dismissing their critics. "Society desperately needs more open scrutiny of scientific claims, not less," says Singal, "whether in scientific journals, the media, or anywhere else."[20]

Yet the publicity persists (grittily). Harvard's Project Implicit still claims on its website that the test "measures attitudes and beliefs that people may be unwilling or unable to report." On its "Ethical Considerations" page, Project Implicit states that "at this stage in its development it is preferable to use the IAT mainly as an educational tool, to develop awareness of implicit preferences and stereotypes"—not only because the test may be unreliable but also because it "sometimes reveals troubling aspects of human nature."[21] In other words, disclaimers notwithstanding, Project Implicit still presents this as a test whose results speak truths that we may not admit to ourselves. Perhaps because of the test's quick results and ease of administration, it has been used at diversity trainings around the world.

The point is not to disparage the idea that racism lies below the surface; it does. But that does not mean that this test reveals hidden truths. By suggesting that it does just that, the researchers manipulate the participants. What if you do not believe the results? The researchers might respond that the results are troubling and that many would rather not face them. Implying that a few clicks can tell you who you are—and that those who contradict the test results must be lying—they deny our capacity to speak for ourselves.

Now that the keystrokes against the IAT are mounting—article upon article, study upon study calling it into question—one might ask why it took so long: why employers and campuses swept it up, why critics stayed in the background, and why it took a few outspoken individuals to bring layers of doubt to the surface. These late rumblings suggest progress. Racism is too serious an issue—with too many layers and manifestations—to reduce to keyboard clicks.

What can be done to combat false research claims and their excessive clout? First, schools, colleges, and scientific institutions and publications can practice precision and skepticism. By teaching reasoning and logic, and by applying these principles to actual studies and reports, schools can help students question the claims that surround them. Teacher preparation programs can do likewise. While encouraging action research, they can warn against its pitfalls; while exposing new teachers to education research, they can encourage cautious interpretation.

Second, researchers can allow themselves more doubt. Instead of aiming for grand conclusions, they can investigate how and why their theories might be incomplete or wrong. Through this redirection, they can help the public understand the questions and working principles.

Third (but not later), the institutions that *popularize* science should adopt more quality control. TED should emphasize substance over "amazingness"; it should bring in speakers who can speak subtly and inconclusively on a range of topics—literature, statistics, music, mathematics, and more. Critique should be part of any intellectual discussion, online or offline; a talk should be judged not by how many hits it gets, but by how well it holds up over time and how the speaker responds to challenge and correction.

In the meantime, anyone who utters the phrase "research has shown" (or any of its variants) should proceed to answer ten questions, for justice's sake: "What research is this?" "Where can I find the published study?" "What do you mean by 'shown'?" "What was the original hypothesis?" "Why did the researchers frame it in this particular way?" "What methods did they use, and why?" "What were the publicized findings?" "What subtleties in the study are not reflected in the abstract or press release?" "What commentary or criticism has the study received?" and "What were the results of any replications?" Then, and only then, will the phrase mean anything at all.

# 6

# SOCIAL AND UNSOCIAL JUSTICE

## How Different Kinds of Justice Combine

In my studies, work, and everyday life, I have often heard people speak of "social justice" as an encompassing good. Many schools and teachers consider social justice their central mission; several high schools in New York City include the phrase in their name (e.g., Community School for Social Justice, Bushwick School for Social Justice, and Nelson Mandela School for Social Justice). It seems harmless, even beneficial, as a phrase and pursuit, yet it lacks something. I look for a landscape but find only a blue puzzle piece.

Yet social justice should not be dismissed as vacuous verbiage. It has a place in any political structure; any social contract entails an understanding of justice for the group. Moreover, through pursuing social justice, an evolving society comes to see which groups it has been favoring over others, and it adjusts accordingly (or not). Social justice is everyone's concern, not just that of its promoters. Even so, it must combine with other justices to have meaning.

When people mention social justice, they rarely associate it with internal life. Social justice is not introspective, except where it involves examining one's attitudes toward a group. It focuses on large-scale problems, not the day-to-day struggles of the heart and mind. To volunteer at a homeless shelter is, by most standards, to contribute to social justice—but to listen to a friend is not, even if the friend is profoundly helped by the act. By everyday, implicit definition, social justice pertains to societal groups and is thus incomplete. Locate it in a greater justice, and it expands; treat it as the ultimate justice, and it shrinks.

To illustrate the limits of social justice, I turn to a twentieth-century Russian poet.

I am grateful that I did not grow up in Russia during the Revolution, but if I had, I would have liked to meet the lumbering Vladimir Mayakovsky, who performed street theater, tossed the past overboard, proclaimed the Revolution, sang communism with full soul, and burgeoned with propaganda. His poetry roared with rebellion; he created new forms, invented new words, and made his life a manifesto. His famous poem "A Cloud in Trousers" begins with a renunciation of hypocrisy and middle-mindedness:

> Your thought,
> dreaming away in a softened brain,
> like a fattened lackey on a greasy sofa,
> I will tease around the blood-soaked rag of my heart;
> brazen and cutting, I will mock my fill.
>
> My soul has not a single grey hair,
> and not a shred of senile tenderness.
> Thundering the world with the might of my voice,
> I walk—handsome,
> twentytwoyearsome. [1]

The Soviet government could not have wished for a better ally—but soon he became too much for them. Censors cut six pages of this very poem and demanded that he change the title (from "The Thirteenth Apostle"). Later on in his career, his plays *The Bedbug* and *The Bathtub* satirized the new society and incensed the Russian Association of Proletarian Writers, who gave him scathing press (and had been harassing him for some time). [2] Mayakovsky committed suicide in 1930. The exact reasons have been debated, yet by the time of his death, he had become a political outsider.

In his complex relationship with Soviet communism, Mayakovsky revealed one of its chief failings. Through pursuit of mass goals, it necessarily cut down the individual. This was not just a result of Soviet power-grabbing; it came with the ideology. A strong individual voice posed a threat *because* it was individual. Many poets (including Alexander Blok, Anna Akhmatova, Marina Tsvetaeva, Osip Mandelshtam, and Boris Pasternak) lived through the Revolution, suffered under the Soviet regime, and resisted it in various ways; Mayakovsky stands out for his energetic and persistent support of the government that turned against him. He brings out the contradictions between different orders of justice.

His communist spirit was consummately individual; even in his solidarity, he stood defiantly alone. His sense of solidarity (not with communists necessarily, but with fellow Futurists) fills the 1912 Futurist manifesto "A Slap in the Face of Public Taste," which he wrote with fellow members of the literary group Hylaea. Full of brazen insults and rhetorical brandishes, this piece declares its disgust with literature as it has been known. "The past is cramped," they write. "Academia and Pushkin are denser than hieroglyphics. Throw Pushkin, Dostoevsky, Tolstoy, etc., etc. off the Ship of Modernity." They likewise discard their contemporaries: "All those Maxim Gorkys, Kuprins, Bloks, Sologubs, Remizovs, Averchenkos, Chornys, Kuzmins, Bunins, etc. etc. need just a dacha on a river. Such is the reward that fate gives to tailors. From the height of skyscrapers we look down on their nothingness!"[3] A tall order, even for the tallest of the Futurists. In fact, Mayakovsky's poetry shows powerful influence from the nineteenth century, as well as resistance to any kind of confinement, even confinement to the terms of the manifesto.

His 1918 poem "Kindness to Horses," or more literally, "A Good Attitude toward Horses," strongly echoes Raskolnikov's dream in the fifth chapter of Dostoevsky's *Crime and Punishment*. Lilya Brik, Mayakovsky's muse and lover, commented on the association between the two works; Pasternak described Mayakovsky's early work as "a kind of continuation of Dostoevsky."[4] In *Crime and Punishment*, Raskolnikov dreams that he is a boy watching a peasant (Mikolka) beat an old mare to death, while others cheer him on. The boy cries, rushes up to her, throws his arms around her, and then rushes at Mikolka and begins beating him with his fists. His father hurries him away as he protests in dismay; Raskolnikov wakes up in a sweat.

In Mayakovsky's poem, the mare falls because of the ice and wind, not because humans beat her—but the people jeer at her in unison, as a unit, as does Kuznetsky Street itself. "A horse has fallen! / Fallen, a horse" / laughed Kuznetsky." The narrator separates himself from the crowd: "I alone / did not mix my voice / into the howl." A little later, he speaks directly to the horse, as tears pour out from him: "Dear horse, please don't. / Sweet horse, listen— / What are you thinking, that you're worse off than they? / Child, / we are all a little bit horse, / each of us a horse in his particular way." The poem goes on from there to a poignant and subtle ending—but these lines bring out the speaker's contradictions, his separation from the crowd even as he finds commonality with others, even with the laughing, even with the horse.[5]

Too idiosyncratic and brilliant to follow a political line, Mayakovsky exemplified the conflict of justices. He devoted himself to social justice, in the form of Soviet communism, and saw it collide with individual justice, or integrity. He championed both, lived them both out, and suffered for this duality, as did many others in different ways. Soviet society was not set up to accommodate the second kind—or even the first.

Any particular form of justice is just a piece of a larger whole—but political and social groups seize and wield the fragments. In public discourse, people take up one kind of justice and dismiss or deride other kinds. The rhetoric becomes ossified and strident. Individualists put down collectivists and vice versa. Yet no one kind of justice can last on its own; without the other kinds, it will collapse on itself.

Through examining different orders of justice, we might come closer to understanding their offerings, limitations, and possible combinations. Let us explore what these justices are and how they can combine.

Let us consider justice at four levels: individual, mutual, social, and public. Public justice differs from social justice in that it seeks a common language across groups.

The word "justice" derives from the Latin *iustitia*, "righteousness, equity," which in turn may derive from the adjective *iustus*, "upright, righteous, equitable," which in turn derives from the proto-Indo-European *yewes-*, "law."[6] To be just is to live by principles of fairness—that is, principles conducive to the good of all. This requires what John Rawls calls "reflective equilibrium"—not a compromise, but a carefully considered calibration of conflicting principles and practices.[7] To weigh and reconcile conflicting goods, one must first identify them. I will begin with individual justice.

Individual justice rests on principles of discernment and internal calibration: seeking and strengthening the good within oneself. Drawing on Plato, one can see it as a microcosm of political and social justice. In his *Republic*, Plato connects self-government (within the individual soul) to the government of a city. The two resemble and relate to each other; in

Plato's view, the justice of a city is *easier* to perceive, since it works on a larger scale. Thus, through examining the city, one can gain insight into the individual.

In Plato's ideal city, the *kallipolis*, it is the philosopher-kings who rule by reason, seeking the good of the city, not their own advantage. It is precisely their learned capacity for reason and deliberation that allows them to rule in this manner. They employ the spirited and appetitive members of the citizenry—essentially the warriors and money-makers, or those with similar impulses—drawing out their good but not letting them take over. In Plato's plan, justice becomes possible when each group performs the role that belongs to it and when reason takes precedence over other impulses.[8]

The soul, likewise, consists of three parts, according to Plato: rational, appetitive, and spirited; reason must rule, but not tyrannically. Appetite and spirit have much to contribute, as long as they do not take over. It is reason that deliberates over the relation of the parts of the soul; "one who is just does not allow any part of himself to do the work of another part or allow the various classes within him to meddle with each other."[9] Like the city, internal government is unselfish; it seeks not personal advantage, not satisfaction of all desires, but the good of the whole. To this end, each part of the soul must do, in proper measure, what it does best.

In contemporary terms, internal justice requires health, yearning, discipline, and discernment. An individual needs health and the conditions that promote and sustain it; without this, he has limited freedom to pursue other goods in life. In addition, an individual needs yearning—the profound longing for something he does not currently have—as well as the liberty to express and act on such yearning without impinging on others. Individual justice requires, above all, discipline and discernment: the restraint of instinct, the practice of working toward goals, and the ability to select among competing desires. A person without discipline will be at the mercy of passions, laziness, and halfhearted attempts; without discernment, he will fall prey to whims, temptations, and outside pressures.

Self-government requires wisdom and imagination—particularly what David Bromwich, taking up a phrase coined by Edmund Burke, calls "moral imagination": the capacity to imagine the consequences of any particular action for one's entire person. "Whether by the ruses of philanthropy, enlightenment, conversion, or war," Bromwich writes, "there is no escaping the question, What shall we be? But even as we ask it, we must admit it to be a weak translation of another question, repeated many times over. Who shall I become?"[10] To rule oneself is to imagine oneself—not only as an actor in the world, but as a shaper of one's own being.

Examples abound in the minute occurrences of a day. Many of us have found ourselves, at one point or another, worrying about the tone of an e-mail we have sent or received, especially since such tone is difficult to discern. Under what circumstances is it right to reply with an inquiry (or follow up with clarification), and when is it better to let the situation go? To determine the right action, we must know ourselves and others, grasp the underlying principles, and apply them to the situation at hand. Each test helps us develop further; even an e-mail exchange can shape character, increase our knowledge, and inform our future actions.

Introspection, too, has necessary limits; a person cannot analyze each act to the depths, or there will be no room for spontaneity and risk. Thus a person must not only examine her own thoughts and actions but at times refrain from doing so, or at least set a bound to such thinking. Thus a person needs not only thought, but various kinds that alternate with each other. There can be no perfect, permanent balance, since the needed proportions vary from one situation to the next. Thus the work of the soul resembles the playing of a musical instrument; some attention goes to the tuning, some to the practice, and some to the play.

Let us now examine the second kind of justice: justice between two. It is characterized by mutuality, even within an uneven or unequal relationship. Not only do the two individuals seek the good together, but they exist in proper relation with each other; that is, their relationship corresponds with their particular responsibilities toward each other and themselves. This proper relation gives dignity to both; neither person tries to gain advantage at the expense of the other. There may be inequality (as between a boss and employee) but no exploitation.

In his *Nicomachean Ethics*, Aristotle holds in highest regard the friendship that pursues and honors the good. According to Aristotle, this kind of friendship is rare because of the virtue and time it requires. Many relationships exist for some third purpose (pleasure or utility), not necessarily the good of either party; this purpose may change or come to an end. Only friendships that pursue the good can be trusted to endure, but they do not come at once. Moreover, the best friendships are based on equality. It is possible for two unequal people to be friends, but only if they act on their proper roles; otherwise they may fall into accusations and quarreling. A friendship based on deception (for instance, when utility is disguised as affection) may come to an end—but the good in a friendship can outlast situational changes.[11]

Drawing on Aristotle, one can find an enduring element even in friendships that come to an end. In modern terms, one can call this dignity. Let us define dignity between two people as (a) a profound equality that transcends a situational inequality; and (b) a recognition of one's own limited knowledge of the self and other. Insofar as the two people can recognize each other's dignity and their own, they maintain mutual justice, a foundation of friendship and other relationships. Yet this dignity slips away all too easily; one person becomes scornful of the other or mistakes a part for the whole. To resist this scorn and diminution is to move toward mutual justice.

A relation of full mutual regard is so rare that it cannot be captured or emulated. The twentieth-century philosopher and theologian Martin Buber suggests this in his description of the "I-You" relation, the relation that involves no containment or possession of the other. It is not an "experience"; it cannot be measured, contained, or willed, but when it occurs, it encompasses everything. Although this relation does not last, its qualities enter our lives. "The It is the eternal chrysalis," Buber writes, "the Thou the eternal butterfly—except that situations do not always follow one another in clear succession, but often there is a happening profoundly twofold, confusedly entangled." Later he writes of the true encounter, "Through the graciousness of its coming and the solemn sadness of its goings it leads you away to the Thou in which the parallel lines of relation meet. It does not help to sustain you in life, it only helps you to glimpse eternity."[12]

In other words, as rare as the "I-You" relation may be, it can nonetheless illuminate relations overall. In the best of circumstances, teachers and students treat each other with regard. The teacher's responsibility is to help the student move toward intellectual independence. Teachers can fall short of this by failing to instruct, growing too attached to (or detached from) their pupils, or treating their pupils as means toward ends (such as test score growth or the "perfect" classroom); even so, they can move toward greater regard. Students, likewise, can move toward regard of their teachers, not by idolizing or disparaging them, but by acknowledging their help, doing their own part, and breaking away when the time comes. The best student-teacher relationship eventually comes to an end (as such) because the student no longer needs the teacher. Student and teacher may remain in touch, even over their lifetimes, but they release the initial relation, which has accomplished its goal, keeping it in memory only. A just relation, in this sense, is aware of its changing form and honors the form that does the most good.

There can be dignity even in a break. Consider a friendship that contains an ongoing misunderstanding—where one person assumes a closer bond or a greater commitment than the other does. Sometimes the friendship can be rescued in these cases; sometimes it cannot. When it cannot, there is honor even in going separate ways, when each one recognizes the worthiness of the other. Now that both understand the situation better than before, they have greater freedom to respond to it and put it in perspective.

In this sense, relations do not exist on their own but take part in larger progressions. We learn from failed friendships and clumsy encounters, and future friendships and encounters reap the benefit. Mistakes keep on coming, but so does the learning.

After these justices, social justice seems limited, even superficial. Yet the other justices cannot exist without it or vice versa. To exercise social justice is to secure a standard of living, including liberty, for a collective. The collective is never fixed; groups merge and dissolve. Individuals join and leave. Still, no matter what the changes, the essential goal of social justice remains the same: to secure and defend the rights of underprivileged groups. This work liberates and limits those involved. Eventually it must include other justices or crumble into nothing.

Martin Luther King Jr.'s "Letter from a Birmingham Jail" (1963) epitomizes social justice that extends to other justices. In this letter, addressed to eight white Alabama clergymen who objected to the nonviolent civil rights protests in Birmingham, King argues that the African American cause is actually part of the great human cause of the centuries. Neither he nor his people are "outsiders," he points out, since injustice affects everyone. Nor is obeying the law an absolute good, since laws are not always just. "A just law," he explains, "is a man-made code that squares with the moral law or the law of God. An unjust law is a code that is out of harmony with the moral law. To put it in the terms of St. Thomas

Aquinas: An unjust law is a human law that is not rooted in the eternal or natural law." Because of this, "injustice anywhere is a threat to justice everywhere"; in breaking the eternal law, it damages humankind. [13]

In quoting from philosophical and religious texts, King emphasizes the gravity and longevity of the civil rights struggle. But he does not rest with the large view; instead, he explores the implications of injustice for the individual. He describes the father who sees his six-year-old daughter's eyes tear up when she learns that she can't go to the amusement park that has been advertised on television and sees "the depressing clouds of inferiority begin to form in her little mental sky." Here King speaks not only of tears and disappointments but of changes to the structure of one's internal being. In addition, he asks his readers to imagine this, to go beyond their usual awareness. His view of justice moves outward and inward; continually searching and questioning, it resists dogma and self-righteousness.

In contrast, some approaches to social justice avoid such searching; they rest on certainty and conviction. But this easy route has dangers. It is easy to adopt a stance in favor of a group's rights; it is harder to be kind to the person standing before us. To avoid the difficulty is to flatten the justice. Any social justice pursued to the exclusion of other justices becomes unjust; it lacks calibration and truth.

The violent student response to Charles Murray's visit to Middlebury College in March 2017 stands as an example of justice gone askew. Murray was invited to Middlebury by the American Enterprise Institute Club to speak on his recent book on class relations. He was widely known (and reviled by many) for his earlier book *The Bell Curve*, which argues, among other things, that genetics play a role in social inequalities. Many were angered by the invitation—not only because they found his views racist but because they saw him as a pseudo-scholar who had been buffered and puffed up by the far right.

When he began speaking, most of the four hundred students in the auditorium rose, turned their backs to him, and began chanting. As they continued to shout him down, it became clear that he would not be able to give his speech. Aware of a possible protest, the hosts and he had already worked out an alternate plan, which he now followed: to move into another room so that he could speak on live stream with Allison Stanger, the professor who originally was to lead the question-and-answer session with him. The relocation did not end the protest. Students crowded into the hallway, shouting and pulling fire alarms; at the end of the interview, when Murray and Stanger attempted to leave, a crowd began pushing them. Someone yanked Stanger's hair and twisted her neck; she ended up with a concussion and neck brace.[14]

Assuming that many of the students were acting on their understanding of social justice—standing up for the rights and dignity of marginalized groups—they were committing injustice against two individuals and against themselves. To shout down a speaker is to deny oneself the education and dignity that comes from listening, even to someone whose views may be flawed and discredited. Even those repulsed by the views can ask, "Who am I, if I must shut out views that offend me?"

The students were perhaps serving one justice at the expense of others. As Stanger points out in her response to the incident, students have seen from President Trump's example that "speech can become action"—that to speak, in many cases, is to wield power over others or to exhibit one's existing power. According to this reasoning, when speech abuses the rights of an oppressed social group, it should be stopped. Yet this argument assumes that all members of a group have identical needs and perspectives; no group is so cohesive. It will have a dissident, or its borders will shift and break. In the case of this incident, some students reported participating uneasily in the protest—or ceasing to participate at a certain point.[15] The actions did not represent everyone present, as individuals or as a body politic. This is the ultimate cost of shutting out a voice; one shuts out one's own as well.

Some of the protesters might have argued: "We believe in free speech, but Murray's talk was not speech. He was invited by a right-wing group with a reactionary agenda. His arguments have long been discredited, but while they lack intellectual weight, they have political power. It is the power and the agenda that we are protesting, not speech itself." Such an argument makes sense—but follow it to its conclusion, and public discourse comes to an end. Most speech comes with an agenda, after all; if we were to focus on the agenda and not the words, there would be no need to listen to anything at all, or so it would seem. In fact, there is great need; speech has the capacity to rise above an agenda, and dialogue— employing what Rawls calls "public reason"—to transcend political divides.[16]

The protesters' actions extend beyond the event. As Stanger points out, the students prevented the larger public from hearing what Murray had to say—which differed from what many assumed he was going to say. Many students and professors protesting Murray's appearance had not read any of his work; they based their objections on hearsay. He was not, as many assumed and chanted, antigay; in fact, he publicly supported gay marriage. Stanger related this misinformation to a larger problem: "Americans today are deeply susceptible to a renunciation of reason and celebration of ignorance. They know what they know without reading, discussing or engaging those who might disagree with them." In Stanger's view, such self-certainty threatens democracy itself. "Our constitutional democracy," she says, "will depend on whether Americans can relearn how to engage civilly with one another."[17] In other words, any social justice must be informed by public justice, justice between two, and justice within the self.

Public justice looks beyond the group to the general public, the assembly of individuals. It consists in the search for and protection of common ground; it allows people to speak to each other in a common language. Insofar as it rests on an understanding of human commonality, it relies on education. Without common knowledge, we have no common language; without common language, there can be no sustained argument. Without sustained argument, our words shrink into puddles of opinion. To exercise public justice, we must work together toward understanding.

Public forums—literary, philosophical, political, artistic, and scientific—can contribute to common knowledge and language. To be "public," they must be open to all and must make room for open dialogue and disagreement. They might take the form of book discussions, debates, policy deliberations, panel discussions of musical compositions, and other events based on common knowledge and interests.

Dialogue sustains and illuminates justice. Without a keen sense of language, we are ill equipped to understand each other and contend with the issues at hand. Through a practice of informed dialogue—not just exchange of opinions, but a common examination of something—we can come to know and see beyond ourselves. But dialogue cannot occur in a void; there must be something to discuss, and the participants must come together with common knowledge and understanding—at least of the nature of the questions at hand.

To prepare oneself for dialogue and discussion, one must recognize the value of such preparation. Those satisfied with their knowledge, those who believe they know more than their adversaries, will see little reason to prepare. Thus public justice requires humility: the recognition that one's own understanding, no matter how advanced, has gaps, errors, and limits.

How does one combine and reconcile the different orders of justice? They not only oppose each other but contain many inherent conflicts and contradictions. By looking at these, we can see justice more finely and broadly.

Individuals will incline more to one kind of justice than another, carrying it into their internal lives, relationships, group struggles, and worldviews. Some seek self-knowledge; others, common cause. All of these tendencies can contribute to a larger justice, if the participants recognize their own pursuits and yearnings as filaments of a larger thread, and that thread of a braid, and the braid of many braids together, with threads breaking off and going their own way. One thread may stand out; it may flash crimson, as in Epictetus's *Discourses*, but it courses through a knotty cloth. Those pursuing one justice must perceive the importance of other kinds.

This is not as easy as it sounds; it involves seeing beyond one's own perspective and preoccupations. Individualists and collectivists have different views of the world; thus they may perceive each other as shallow or selfish. They may even feel that the other is impinging on them, imposing a view of the world that doesn't fit. To pursue justice, one must acknowledge those who differ profoundly from us yet work in their own way for the good. We do not have to become them, but we can meet them with respect.

On an ordinary evening in college, for example, one student might decide to focus on study, another might attend a political meeting, and another might meet with a friend to reconcile after a misunderstanding. None of these actions is automatically superior to the others. The one who devotes the evening to studies may end up with lasting knowledge, understanding, and discipline. The one who attends the political action meeting may learn about things happening in the world and find ways to support or resist them. The one who meets with a friend may repair a relationship.

Once people understand the importance of other views, they combine justices more easily. Suppose two people in a workplace have conflicting attitudes toward recycling. One of the two believes that the recycling should be doubled and tripled and that this will require peer monitoring.

That is, every work area should have a designated monitor who observes and records his colleagues' recycling habits. Another resents the intrusion of privacy and feels that people should be trusted to recycle on their own without being monitored. Clearly both are right; recycling requires vigilance, and workplaces benefit from trust. To honor both goods, they could remove personal trash bins (so that everyone disposes of trash in designated areas) and then keep an eye on the bins themselves. If people are disposing of items improperly, then they might track down the culprits; otherwise they will leave people alone. This solution involves group justice, individual justice, and justice between two (in this case, the two colleagues, who observe a respectful collegial relation).

We are far from attaining such combination and mutual regard; especially in politics, we tend to pit ourselves against the perceived "other side." The problem escalated with the 2016 presidential election but did not originate with it. According to a 2014 Pew study, Americans are more polarized politically than they have been in the previous two decades. They have more antagonism toward the opposing party; they see their opponents as not only wrong but dangerous. Moreover, the most vociferous citizens tend to be the ones at the extremes; moderates have declined in number and generally keep a lower profile.[18] In other words, we have a country of people yelling at and past each other. This does not and cannot lead to justice. It does not even lead to good grammar.

Ancient texts wrestle with justice's complexity. The Hebrew Bible presents justice as a kind of mental clarity and impartiality—yet this idea immediately runs into problems. In Deuteronomy 16:19 (JPS translation), Moses tells the Israelites, "You shall not judge unfairly: you shall show no partiality; you shall not take bribes, for bribes blind the eyes of the discerning and upset the plea of the just." This sounds reasonable, except that partiality has filled the story of the Israelites—from Abraham, who favored Isaac over Ishmael; to Isaac, who favored Esau over Jacob (but whom Jacob tricked into blessing him); to Jacob, who favored Joseph, to the bitter resentment of Joseph's brothers; to Moses himself, whom God singled out. Favoritism is now to be avoided, but it is also permanently present—in the Israelites' ancestry and understood destiny. Thus even this simple definition of justice contains tensions, contradictions, and impossibilities. This may be the greatest lesson of all: that no justice can be glib or easy. At some point, justice goes against something dear to us.

Of the justices, social justice currently runs the greatest risk of going glib; people speak of it too frequently and easily, as though everyone knew what it was or should be. Like any justice, social justice has meaning only within the difficulties; to evade them is to evade justice itself. If there is to be a school of social justice, let there also be a neighboring school of individual justice, and let them come together to discuss ethical and political problems.

It will be a glistening day when we no longer hear of social justice alone, or individual justice alone, but of justices in combination, each one drawing on different subjects, people, and exigencies. Yet within that complexity and panoply, there will be an overarching justice: the justice of taking oneself in measure, of knowing that one does not possess full knowledge of the good but must seek it continually. Through diligent seeking, people come face-to-face; through tilts of view, they see beyond arrogance.

# 7

# THE TOXICITY OF "TOXIC"

Our bookshelves and websites bulge with writings on "toxic" people and how to keep them at bay. Titles include Dr. Lillian Glass's *Toxic People: Ten Ways of Dealing with People Who Make Your Life Miserable* (1995); David Gillespie's *Taming Toxic People: The Science of Identifying and Dealing with Psychopaths at Work and at Home* (2017); Susan Forward and Craig Buck's *Toxic Parents: Overcoming Their Hurtful Legacy and Reclaiming Your Life* (2002); Liz Ryan's opinion piece "How to Get Toxic People Out of Your Life" (*Forbes*, June 15, 2017); Marcel Schwantes's "Six Toxic Types of People You Need to Cut from Your Life Right Now" (*Inc.*, February 9, 2017); and hundreds along similar lines. These works propose a grand disinfection; with the right psychological spray, they claim, we could rid the air of all noxious elements—that is, toxic people—and emerge safe and sound. This is profound and damaging nonsense; it harms not only the so-called toxic people, not only the people who deal with them, but our conception of human relations. [1]

The perceived problem has some traces of reality. There are people who hurt others, not only lightly but seriously, not only once but over and over. There are people who make their workplaces unpleasant, who spoil social gatherings, or who put a strain on all their friends and family members. There are those who seek strategically to get as much out of others as possible, spreading malicious rumors, manipulating emotions, and abusing their own power or charisma; there are those who rape and kill. But many supposedly "toxic" people fall far short of this; they pose an inconvenience but not a true threat. Using the term "toxic" carelessly not only lumps all inconveniences together but justifies the act of writing people off.

"A toxic person," writes Glass, "is anyone who has poisoned your life, who is not supportive, who is not happy to see you grow, to see you succeed, who does not wish you well. In essence, he or she sabotages your efforts to lead a happy and productive life." Right there, Glass's argument reveals incongruities; a person who "is not supportive" or "does not wish you well" has not necessarily "sabotaged your efforts" at happiness or productivity. None of us is the center of all existence; not all frowns are directed our way. Even if they were, they wouldn't have to destroy us. Nor are we obliged to cheer everyone on; the subdued audience member may have more room to listen and think. Presumably we can grow strong enough not to need universal applause. Those who do not support us may have things to teach us, directly or indirectly; they may help tilt our attention to something beyond our immediate hopes and dreams. Glass's "toxic" presumes a humanity allergic to itself. [2]

She identifies "thirty types of toxic terrors": among them, the "Cut-You-Downer," the "Chatterbox," the "Gossip," the "Gloom and Doom Victim," the "Jokester," the "Unconscious Social Klutz," the "Penny-Pinching Miser," the "Competitor," the "Accusing Critic," the "Emotional Refrigerator," and the "Skeptical Paranoid." She warns readers that they "may be surprised to recognize many people [they] know, and whom [they] may not like, in the categories." The offending behaviors range from "backhanded compliments" to "free-flowing stream of consciousness," from worrying to continual joking. The author's own judgments appear at times more obnoxious than the "toxic" behaviors themselves; she says of "Unconscious Social Klutzes" that they "usually have poor eye contact, poor posture, poor handshakes, poor vocal intonation, and poor social graces." Skeptical paranoids, in her description, "often have doubting looks on their faces and usually seem to be hesitating as they throw cold water on every idea you have." Glass does not consider that people may simply be imperfect; imperfection, in this scheme, calls for a nickname, a type, and a taunt. [3]

Yet Glass's book, for all its judgmentalism, appears generous in comparison to other writings. In prescribing ways of dealing with toxic types, she at least finds room for engagement of some kind; many others advise readers simply to cut the so-called toxic people from their lives. In her article "Seven Tips for Eliminating Toxic People from Your Life," Zoe

Weiner insists that if you give these people the slightest chance, they will take advantage of it and use you all over again. She quotes Tara Mackey, the author of *Cured by Nature*, who claims that toxic people "will use any weakness over time to sneak back into your life."[4] According to Weiner and Mackey, anyone who distracts you from your "positive and productive habits" (with the possible exception of depressed people) can be considered toxic—and toxic people cannot be trusted in any way. They need the firmest and most absolute of boundaries.

Such a claim erroneously presumes that we would all be positive and productive from morning to night if we just cut those horrible people out of our lives. It ignores the possibility that we are all mixtures of things: that we go through easy and difficult times; that we sometimes need others more, sometimes less; and that we may need time to get to know each other. Moreover, people may carry more goodwill and consideration than others recognize; the supposedly toxic person, far from trying to manipulate and control everything, far from holding his or her needs above everyone else's, may have a kinder soul than anyone knows. Because of cultural and generational differences, as well as the complexities of personality, it is easy to misjudge someone at the outset or even for a long time. But to understand others, we must perceive our own weaknesses. Weiner and Mackey call for a barrier between the healthy and unhealthy, as though we could be divided so cleanly into two camps and as though, by scratching others off a list, we could attain happiness. These and other authors advocate shallow judgment, not justice.

Often the judgment is premature if not utterly wrong. Schwantes advises people to "cut ties with people who kiss up to management":

> They will go out of their way to befriend and manipulate management in order to negotiate preferential treatment—undue pay raises, training, time off, or special perks that nobody else knows about or gets. Keep an eye out for colleagues who spend way more face time with their managers than usual. The wheels of favoritism may be in motion. Time to cut ties.[5]

Why should anyone assume that a person who speaks at length with management is trying to "negotiate preferential treatment"? Such conversations could have myriad reasons and motives, some ethically grounded, others not. Instead of "cutting ties," we might be better off suspending judgment. Long conversations, even with management, are not necessarily evil.

Where does this notion of "toxic people" come from? Glass is credited with coining the phrase, but "toxic person" dates at least two decades before her book. The concept has an even longer history.[6]

The word "toxic" derives from the Late Latin *toxicus*, "poisoned," which in turn derives from the Greek *toxikon pharmakon*, "poison for use on arrows." *Toxikon*, the neuter of *toxikos*, means "pertaining to arrows or archery."[7] Originally designating something not only poisonous but deadly, the word today suggests fierce and ubiquitous threat. Worse than poison, it has no salutatory aspect; yet omnipresent, it adheres to everything human, as though the human race itself were venomous. Doom is nigh; if we are to believe the guides, we breathe toxic air just by being around others. The only way to save ourselves is to quarantine these terrible people, to erect walls so strong and dense that not even their breath can cross over.

Toxic people, according to these writers, come in breathtaking variety. There's the toxic friend who needs company, the toxic aunt who breaks secrets, the toxic date who keeps calling after you have said you're not interested, the toxic sibling who drinks. There's the toxic supervisor who talks about her personal life at meetings, the toxic employee who picks arguments (or tries too hard to make peace), the toxic stranger who smiles at you on the train (or fails to smile), the toxic tenant who always has a reason for being late with rent (or leaves notes reminding people not to clutter the hallways). There's the toxic salesperson, the toxic customer, the toxic cabdriver, the toxic passenger—why, toxicity is everywhere except in you. With few exceptions, writers on this topic proclaim the goodness of the self. The self would be boundless, successful, pure, were it not for those awful individuals.

Yet if you approached each of these deadly people—asked them a few questions, came to know them a little—you would find yourself still alive and in reasonable health, perhaps healthier than before. Some of them have a harmless quirk or two. Others have a difficult life circumstance that makes them morose. Still others have bad habits. Only a few poison their surroundings—and then it's rarely all their own doing.

Why, then, the tendency to call so many people "toxic"?

It fits within a general worldview (particularly American, though found also in other cultures) that each of us directs our own success and happiness—that if we just keep our eye on the goal and clear away all obstacles, we shall achieve our dreams. Those who fall short of their goals have failed *spiritually* or *psychologically*; perhaps they do not believe enough in themselves (or God), or perhaps they let others stand between them and their aspirations. Those of us who believe in ourselves should never flail (according to the dictum); no matter what toxins get hurled at us, we will raise up our shields and gleam in our own empowerment. These hurled toxins often take the form of other people; no matter how noble or generous our strivings, someone will fly splat into them. It is on us, then, as believers, to build good protections and sensors.

Here the self-help writers have gone wrong. Yes, to reach a goal, one must often overcome obstacles (and even ward off toxins), but these are usually circumstances, not individuals. Humans contain so much history and possibility, so many varied and contradictory elements, that only rarely do they harm with their entire being. Most of us have agreeable and disagreeable qualities; most of us help and hinder. In addition, sometimes through our quirks we offer the most, through startling others into questioning.

"Toxic" is not just a benign misnomer; it affects human dignity. It even has a toxic effect. Once a person is deemed "toxic" and identified by type and subclass, there is no reason to get to know him or her; the person is best avoided or skillfully manhandled. A toxic man says nothing that matters; if you take his ideas seriously, you will fall for his tricks. A toxic woman has gotten away with far too much for too long, at our expense; so we must push her away and reclaim what is ours, once and for all, and do the same with all her kind. A "toxic" person belongs to a substratum of humanity (or exists entirely outside of the human race).

A toxic person poisons those in the vicinity; therefore, those remaining close to him or her (physically or emotionally) must be toxic too. Thus the word casts aspersions on an entire group. When, in August 2017, President Trump tweeted that the Arizona senator Jeff Flake was "toxic," he dismissed not only Flake but (implicitly) any Flake supporters and anyone who, in Trump's view, could be deemed "weak" in ideology or following: "Great to see that Dr. Kelli Ward is running against Flake Jeff Flake, who is WEAK on borders, crime and a non-factor in Senate. He's toxic!"[8] However tempting it may be to call Trump "toxic" in return, this recycles the existing problems and adds new ones. "Standing near something toxic for too long is lethal," writes Rex Huppke in the *Chicago Tribune*. "And I don't think the Republican Party wants to die."[9] It would be better argued that standing too close to Trump puts a person in a moral predicament (which he or she then has to resolve). Those close to Trump in one way or another—that is, those who work with him, associate with him, share his views, or support him—have not automatically been poisoned; they retain the ability to choose their actions.

Trump is so intolerant of dissenters, so insistent on his own way, that the word "toxic" almost applies to him. But one can get stuck in this word; sloppy language breeds sloppy language. Calling him toxic does no good and can even encourage a "toxic" mudfight. It does more good to look at where Trump came from, who supports him and why, and what troubles and conflicts roil the nation.

Careless language lets us off the hook. If we can dismiss others as toxic, we need not bother to understand them or those around them. This leads to great loss—not only the loss of these particular people but our own internal loss, the loss of willingness to deal with difficulty. If I have a coworker who continually asks what I think of her work, if I hear from others that she seeks their approval at every possible occasion, I do not have to dismiss her as needy and cloying. At some point, I can take her aside and say, "I see that you want to know what I think of your work, but I am not in a position to evaluate it all the time, nor do I have that kind of authority." Or else I might consider the situation as a whole; is there enough helpful critique in the workplace, or is it lacking? In the latter situation, I might propose some kind of structure for peer critique. Perhaps this person is not alone in wanting to hear from colleagues; perhaps she is not displaying a personal problem but revealing an institutional lack.

Or imagine a graduate school setting where one student has a reputation for viciousness. He spreads rumors about who is favored by the professors, who has the greatest chance of getting a high-prestige position, and so forth. It would be easy to brand him toxic and have nothing to do with him. But if he is spreading rumors, the chances are high that others listen to them. Instead of pointing the finger at him, the students in question can look at their own behavior and priorities. If they have been taking part in gossip, perhaps it is time to redirect their focus. Gossip distracts—and by its nature cannot come from one person alone. Perhaps this instigator, no longer having an audience, must now speak about something else; perhaps he has interesting things to say, and perhaps his fellow students, by redirecting their own conversation, can learn from him and each other.

Just as on the national scale, just as at work and school, we can avoid writing people off in personal life, as this shortchanges not only them but us. To an extent, we choose our friendships and romantic relationships; even our mistakes form part of our character and understanding. Friends, once close, find themselves diverging—yet in explaining this to themselves and others, they do not have to descend into the vile. "Then I realized she was toxic"—this demeans not only the other person but the friendship and, with it, the self. Problems arise in relationships: one person may become too busy or too possessive, a misunderstanding may drag on for too long, or the bond itself may end. All of this can be handled graciously, most of the time—and when it cannot, the language can.

Kind language need not gloss over reality; it describes the self and others as accurately and considerately as possible, making room for the unknown. In this regard, whoever uses such language honors both the self and others. Mean language makes me mean; generous language suggests dimension. My remarks about others even affect my character, on the spot; in making room for others, I make room for myself. "Toxic" makes no room.

The word "toxic" not only shrinks the self but contributes to what David Brooks calls a "siege mentality": the notion that a noble few of us are beset by enemies in our everyday lives—in our schools, workplaces, homes—and that only by crying out our victimhood, only by pointing out the abusers, can we achieve some kind of vindication. [10] Such self-victimization and self-sequestration allows for no conversation with others; it presumes and relies on camps of good and evil. Were the enemy to prove complex, even partly good, then the victims' victimhood would come apart, and with it, their identity. But complexity allows for a hardier identity in the end. Recognizing complexity does not entail denying abuse; one can name abuse while perceiving in everyone the capacity for good and harm. Seeing ourselves as fallible, we not only slow down in condemning others, but recognize gradations of fault and hurt. Not all abuses are alike; some are slips of the moment, others the violence of years.

What words and phrases can take the place of "toxic"? Anything more specific and less reckless, with appropriate distribution of responsibility, would be an improvement. Suppose a coworker comes in late every day, seems perennially in need of coffee, and spends most of the day gossiping. The boss should address the lateness; the coffee is the responsibility of the person in question, and the gossiping takes at least two. If those affected take care of their own part, at least some of the problem will shrivel. Instead of calling the person toxic, one can acknowledge that many people together let a permissive situation get out of hand. Or consider a relative who takes each family gathering as an opportunity to show off—but genuinely enjoys seeing everyone. The others can recognize the person's genuineness but set a limit to the showing off (or else indulge it, if they wish).

Some will protest the apparent naiveté of this argument, pointing to the cases of people who commit harm despite all restraints against them: child molesters, murderers, wife-beaters, violent racists, peeping Toms, slanderers, and others at similar levels of depravity. Yet even here, there is nothing to be gained from the vagueness of "toxic"; something more direct and specific would bring swifter resolution. "We have a toxic neighbor" tells the police nothing; "We have a neighbor who spies on us" says a bit more and may help bring the behavior to an end. If a teenage boy possesses guns and intends to use them against classmates at school, then much more good is done by stating so than by calling him toxic.

Others may object that I am imposing formal standards on an informal word: that "toxic" was never meant seriously but instead belongs in the same register as "amazing" and "terrible." If we make all our language formal, they note, it will lose its spontaneity and verve. This argument would have weight if "toxic" clearly belonged to informal speech. Instead, it has spilled into other registers: not only into books, articles, and speeches, but also into psychology and its popular counterparts. Books about "toxic" people claim the authority of the social sciences; far from admitting to informality, they drape themselves in robes of scholarship.

Still others will point out that "toxic" is just one word among many in current use, that protesting it is like railing against a raindrop. I stand not against the isolated word, though, but against its accompanying torrent: the phrases and words that we pelt and get pelted by, hour after hour, trend after trend. Hesitation stands higher than careless words of this kind. We do not have to characterize everything right away; if the right words do not come immediately, we can often afford to wait.

Still other defenders of "toxic" protest that it's a metaphor. Metaphors abound in our speech; why get so riled up over them? To this I reply, using another metaphor, that metaphors run the gamut. They can be beautiful, hideous, meaningful, empty; some metaphors open up our understanding, while others shut it down. This particular metaphor shuts down not only our understanding but our perception; if we use it without regard for appropriateness, we become less sharpened to the world. A metaphor does not get a free pass to the tongue; words and phrases, no matter how figurative, still need to pass through the mind.

These arguments may seem laborious to the purveyors of self-help, who concern themselves not with words but with solutions that sell. If the word "toxic" in a title attracts a customer's eye, if the customer then buys the book and finds it useful, hasn't everyone won? A book's commercial success, however, has little to do with its quality; a top-selling life solution may quickly fall apart. To illustrate this I will turn not to self-help, not even to psychology, but to two works of literature by authors of great imagination, independence, and wit. "What does literature have to tell us?" some might ask. "It's made up, after all." Yes, and those made-up things can provoke us to see our lives and particular situations in a new way. Without bringing in spoilers or long quotes, I will briefly consider George Saunders's story "Winky" and László Krasznahorkai's *Herman* (two interrelated short stories, "The Game Warden" and "The Death of a Craft"). My fractional descriptions are meant only to hint at the works and the possibilities they uncover.

In Saunders's "Winky," eighty people have gathered at the Hyatt for a life-changing event in which they enact the mantra "Now Is the Time for Me to Win." Employing a confusing succession of metaphors, the presenters act out an individual, "You," struggling for Inner Peace and overcoming such obstacles as self-absorption, depression, and blame. Suddenly, through a deft twist, the obstacles become other people; Tom Rodgers, the leader, explains that other people "come up and crap in your oatmeal all the time"—and the key to success is to "screen off your metaphorical oatmeal" so that people can't do that anymore. He calls on people to line up for a change—"A *dramatic* change." Neil Yaniky rises and gets in line. [11]

Before learning who his personal obstacle is, before learning what he plans to do and what comes of his resolution, we stand in weirdly familiar waters. Without having attended such a meeting before, we know it well; from many corners, we hear the message that we *should* be attaining success—and if we are not doing so, we have only ourselves to blame—but—here again the twist—our main fault lies in letting *others* get in our way. So this success formula justifies cruelty; if others, through their personality, actions, or sheer existence, have prevented us from going where we want to go, then we have not only the right but the obligation—according to such teaching—to push them aside and move on.

In turning the obstacles into human beings, Tom Rodgers and his helpers make the project of success both meaner and more viscerally satisfying. To realize my goals in life, all I have to do is put the brake on those external annoyances. If Person X is gone, maybe I will be able to associate with Persons Y and Z, who look better, dress better, have nicer things, and can do more for me. Maybe I can rise to my intended station in the world, which must be higher than my current one. This requires no work beyond the act of cutting people off, "putting a screen on the oatmeal," as it were. Because it is so easy, it has more appeal than introspection; it can be accomplished in a few minutes (by those who have worked up the will).

The rest of the story shows how this plays out; it holds surprises no matter what the reader's expectations might be. The ending does not have a single meaning; it leaves us with puzzle and trouble. Something was wrong all along, and something was not; we are left to figure out what.

Krasznahorkai's *Herman* concerns a game warden tasked with the duty of trapping and killing the "noxious predators"—wolves, foxes, stray dogs, feral cats, badgers, and such—that have been ravaging the farms. He begins zestily but soon finds himself in a crisis of truth. The phrase "noxious predators" and its variants ring falser and falser until Herman brings the affair to an end; the two stories, telling different versions, leave us uncertain of the meaning. In both, Herman wreaks revenge, but how, and against whom? And how does he conclude, or how do others conclude him? The indefiniteness breaks up our happy answers. No matter what our interpretations, we must disbelieve in the phrase "noxious predators"—for if Herman himself has become noxious through his disbelief in this phrase, then what is it, really, but a call to conformity, a call that only a few dare to resist? In breaking away from his assignment, Herman becomes terminally unpleasant; not only that, but he and Krasznahorkai together upbraid anyone who would brand him as noble. There's nothing noble about him, nothing possessable or malleable—for what we hold up high we also claim, and Herman will not be owned. The stories throw us out of our domains; losing our possessions momentarily, we turn our eyes to the night. But soon that, too, will tire us; we will turn back, like the characters, to cushions and chocolate, to our ways of explaining the world. All the same, language shifts and breaks. If we gain something definite from this literature, it is an exhilarating release from the surety of words. [12]

I am not going to tack on any perfunctory "studies have shown" statement. This is my study: a study of words. It takes "toxic" and gives it a good shaking, only to see it crumble, most of the time, into dust. If we took time to reconsider the dismissive language flying all around, our words and relations would gain dignity—not the dignity of stuffed-up or timorous speech, but that of recognition, of seeing something of ourselves, and something beyond ourselves, in others.

Questioning the word "toxic" does not mean turning it into taboo, making it one of those things that "we just don't say." Rather, in making it less automatic, we enliven thought and feeling; we come to see people as more than we know. In this way we detoxify our own attitudes and prepare ourselves for long life. If anything makes long life worthwhile, it is the awareness that there is more to come, not only in the world, but in the mind; not only on grandiose occasions, but each morning, over coffee or on the train. Not only do we have more to learn, but the learning fills our days.

# 8

# THE SPRINGS OF CREATIVITY

## How Invention and Creation Require Subject Matter

The trumpets have blasted: it is time to instill more creativity in our schools, workplaces, and life. Without it, experts say, we will fall behind personally and economically; our gifts will go to waste and our structures will crumble. Thus the Partnership for 21st Century Learning has named creativity "the premier skill of the 21st century"; the Organization for Economic Co-operation and Development describes a new "creative economy" that calls for a "new paradigm" of education, in which the old bureaucracy will be replaced by an open, adaptive, dynamic system. American creativity is on a dangerous decline, experts warn; it is time to meet the "creativity crisis" head-on.[1] But there are contradictions in these calls; their dogma defies creativity itself. Creativity cannot be institutionalized; the best way to promote it is to give it room and substance. An inventor creates new things not by "being creative" but by finding new solutions to problems. This requires long, stubborn, springy work: a willingness to test something to the limit, even if no one else deems it relevant.

Those calling for a creativity revolution cite the pressing needs of the era. Today's workers, they say, must possess technical and personal skills; they must be able to change direction at a moment's notice, adapt quickly to changing conditions, and collaborate within complex networks. A poetry translator or jazz pianist might have exceptionally high creativity, but not the kind wanted here; even a theoretical physicist would miss the mark. The Council on Competitiveness calls for science education precisely because of the number of technical jobs in today's market. (One wonders whether those with science backgrounds would even find such positions satisfying.) "The number of jobs requiring technical training is growing at five times the rate of other occupations," they state, and "U.S. high school students underperform most of the world on international math and science tests"; therefore "the nation must take deliberate steps to expand the pool of technical talent."[2] Something other than creativity and innovation is at stake here; the Council on Competitiveness seems mainly concerned with employment (and competitiveness, as its name suggests). Market competitiveness fuels certain kinds of innovation but ignores others.

Skeptics ask whether those clamoring for creativity, in business and elsewhere, really want it at all. Barry Staw wrote in 1995 that "although there is practically a cottage industry devoted to celebrating successful innovations and touting their characteristics as the 'new solution,' few managers really want to pay the price for innovation." In fact, organizations "work very hard to recruit and select employees who look and act like those already in the firm" and spend resources socializing those new hires who do not quite fit in.[3] Much of the creativity clamor may be hot air. The old, surly kind of creativity, the kind that tinkers with things late into the night, would not be welcomed in the "creative economy," the "knowledge economy," or any other epithets of the times. Such creativity ruminates and resists; it comes out through the edges and cracks of thought.

Tests of creativity—whose scores are cited as evidence of the crisis— have biases and limitations. The Torrance Tests (created by Ellis Paul Torrance, who cautioned against the use of composite scores) involve both verbal and figural tasks. For some of the latter, students must arrange shapes into new pictures, which are then scored for creativity. These tasks are supposed to measure fluency, elaboration, originality, resistance to premature closure, and abstractness of titles. It is questionable whether (a) they actually measure such qualities and (b) these qualities truly constitute creativity. Some people have difficulty generating ideas on the spot; their best ideas come over time, after they have been mulling over a problem or idea. Also, originality can be blatant or subtle; while a subtler kind may not get recognized on a test, it might ultimately result in a magnificent work. For the other matter, there is more to creativity than the qualities listed here; creativity also involves turning a subject or problem around in the mind. The Torrance Test—and other tests of its kind—may favor those who respond quickly and profusely to test questions—in other words, expert brainstormers. This is far from the whole of creativity.[4]

Creativity is the mental state and process that results in creation of new things. To create new things, one often pushes up against existing models; testing out and working with possibilities, one responds to what has come before and anticipates what may follow. Thus creativity requires not just surface knowledge but detailed insight into structure. From that perspective, the best way to promote creativity is to teach subject matter and encourage experimentation within it. This requires not so much a revolution as a practice of study and play within the disciplines. Why, then, the brass alarm? Why the dire assessment? Why the call for total overhaul? I will examine the roots of this purported crisis and propose a different understanding of creativity: the habits, inclinations, and practices of working within a discipline and pushing beyond its limits.

Theories of creativity emphasize its close relation to subject matter. Alfred North Whitehead, credited with coining the term "creativity," considered it the underlying principle of existence, transcending both the abstract and the concrete. "The definiteness of fact is due to its forms," he wrote; "but the individual fact is a creature, and creativity is the ultimate behind all forms, inexplicable by forms, and conditioned by its creatures." According to Whitehead, creativity comes out of a meeting of old and new, where the individual, confronting the known, casts it in new form: "In this process the creativity, universal throughout actuality, is characterized by the datum from the past; and it meets this dead datum—universalized into a character of creativity—by the vivifying novelty of subjective form selected from the multiplicity of pure potentiality. In the process, the old meets the new, and this meeting constitutes the satisfaction of an immediate particular individual."[5] For the old and new to come together, something of the old must be known.

Other theories of creativity—such as honing theory, which views creativity as a response to entropy—likewise emphasize creativity's intricate involvement with subject matter.[6] It cannot exist in a void, or even in speculation or brainstorming. It comes through long relationship with natural phenomena, language, technology, and art. Thus it exists in time; its best work might not be on the spot, at a meeting or on a test, but in late-night brooding, long morning walks, and sudden thoughts at 2:23 p.m. and other odd and even moments of the day.

Those who name a creativity crisis, and call for a creativity revolution, draw on self-help and corporate cultures. Like self-help writers and speakers, they profess that each of us carries a great gift that only needs proper release. "Everyone has huge creative capacities," writes Sir Ken Robinson. "The challenge is to develop them."[7] This sounds exciting, but what does "huge" mean? Must everyone attain fame and wealth or accomplish something momentous, or do modest creative contributions count? Is it not enough to do well in a profession that one enjoys? The hyperbole of the statement could easily give people the jitters.

For all his rhetoric, Robinson acknowledges the importance and specificity of subject matter. In contrast, many self-help books treat subject matter as irrelevant. The specifics do not matter, according to the gurus, since the basic principles apply to everyone. Look within. Draw up lists. See what moves and excites you. Shed all those negative beliefs that hold you back, and go for your dreams. In *The Courage to Be Creative*, bestselling author Doreen Virtue advises readers to "be open to all possibilities, noticing ideas without censoring them or worrying whether they're feasible. Don't just think outside the box . . . think like there *is* no box!"[8] In *Creative Confidence: Unleashing the Creative Potential within Us All*, Tom Kelley and David Kelley argue exactly what the book's title suggests: that through building our creative confidence, we become the creative selves we always were. "At its core," they write, "creative confidence is about believing in your ability to create change in the world around you. It is the conviction that you can achieve what you set out to do. We think this self-assurance, this belief in your creative capacity, lies at the heart of innovation."[9] Such books dole out spoonfuls of sweetened and softened truth. They suggest that all you need for creativity is an open mind and a good feeling, the recipe for many a bad poem.

Over a century ago, G. K. Chesterton parodied this ethos of self-belief in "The Fallacy of Success"; his mockery continues to ring true. "You may want to jump or to play cards," he writes, "but you do not want to read wandering statements to the effect that jumping is jumping, or that games are won by winners. If these writers, for instance, said anything about success in jumping it would be something like this: 'The jumper must have a clear aim before him. He must desire definitely to jump higher than the other men who are in for the same competition. He must

let no feeble feelings of mercy (sneaked from the sickening Little Eng-
landers and Pro-Boers) prevent him from trying to *do his best*. He must
remember that a competition in jumping is distinctly competitive, and
that, as Darwin has gloriously demonstrated, THE WEAKEST GO TO
THE WALL.'"[10] Such "wandering statements" abound in the creativity
literature; it is as though the creativity writers believed that an attitude of
success could bring forth a symphony.

Corporate statements, too, reflect a limited and misleading notion of
creativity. In their idea-generation phases, companies often use a win-
nowing process: they welcome many initial ideas, then select the ones
that they can use. Thus "creativity," in the business context, means different things at different levels. The regular worker, whether asked to brain-
storm or to work out an idea in detail, contributes only one possible idea
to the pile. Microsoft's CIO Tony Scott explains, "We encourage innovation. But we quickly settle on those things that are going to make a
difference and weed out those things that are not going to make a difference."[11] At Amazon, an engineer with an idea may be invited to pitch it to
the executive committee; Jeff Bezos decides on the spot whether to explore it. If it's a go, a small team experiments with it; if the experiments
prove successful, the company may take the idea further.[12] While such
practices make sense for the company, they conflict with the basic creative principles of self-reliance, independence of others' judgment, and
long persistence.

As a result, when people in corporate contexts talk about creativity,
they refer not to the long, disciplined process of creating something new,
but to a team effort that elicits and discards hundreds of ideas along the
way. To participate well in such a process, an employee must be willing
to generate initial ideas and then let go of them. This is not creativity but
a gyration of the mind.

A different view of creativity could enliven school curricula, tone down a
few fads, and inform public discussion. Such creativity starts with tinkering within a topic or problem. The person already knows a given form—a
sonnet, a geometric proof, a computer program, an essay—and wishes to
take it in a new direction. He or she may begin with a slight variation or
extension, seeing what it brings and where it goes. This leads to other
extensions and experiments, conducted with attention to the whole. This

work requires concentration and solitude, as well as complex collaboration.

For an example, I bring up my great-grandfather Max Fischer's oldest brother, Charles Fischer, a toolmaker, spring-maker, and inventor. Through his work with springs, he came to know their properties; through knowing their properties, he saw how to test them out in new contexts and apply them to everyday problems. I present here three of his inventions: a telephone stand, a take-up spring, and a book prop. I never met Charles Fischer, as he died almost two decades before I was born. I knew nothing about him until a few years ago. As I began learning more, I found that he knew his field and took it in new directions. As the founder and head of the spring company, he responded to market demands and attained prosperity, yet he also played with possibilities that could not have been lucrative.

Charles Fischer came to the United States from Hungary around 1890, at age fourteen, with his parents, Sigmund and Fanny Fischer, and seven siblings, Lena, William, Sam, Frieda, Max, David, and Emanuel. During their first ten years, they lived in the Lower East Side of Manhattan; they later branched out to Brooklyn, upper Manhattan, and Queens. Charles never attended school in America, as far as I know; he worked first as a toolmaker, then as a spring-maker. This work experience gave him the necessary background for his career.

In 1906 he founded the Chas. Fischer Spring Company (which produced the AN-6530 goggles used by U.S. Navy and Army flight crews during World War II). While running the company (and employing family members—my great-grandfather was the bookkeeper), he invented and patented many devices, ranging from coat racks to goggle parts to a speedometer. Most of his inventions involved a spring of some kind; its repeated occurrence suggests a mind playing with variations and ideas.

The phrase "mechanical spring" typically refers to a coil, but the category encompasses a range of elastic devices that store mechanical energy, from the bow to the rubber band to the gas spring. Springs conform approximately to Hooke's law, first stated by Robert Hooke in 1676 in the form of a Latin anagram, *ceiiinosssttuu*, whose solution is *Ut tensio, sic vis* ("As the tension, so the force").[13] This law states that the force needed to compress or extend a spring is proportional to the distance of compression or extension. The law applies only to distances within a given range, and then only approximately; if the spring is extended or compressed too far, it will become distorted, and even with proper use, all springs are subject to wear and tear. Even so, the law has proven fundamental to mechanical engineering and has informed the construction of clocks, spring scales, and other devices.

Fischer's telephone stand, take-up spring, and book prop employ coil springs; the book prop uses a spring clamp as well. Shaped like a helix, the coil spring has a natural length to which it reverts when released; some coil springs are designed to resist compression, others to resist expansion. The design must suit the purpose precisely.

None of these inventions is entirely new; each one improves on similar inventions or inventions directed at a similar end. Thus Fischer needed not only knowledge of springs, not only a fascination with everyday problems, but familiarity with existing technology. Beneath each invention, one hears the question: "How can I improve on the existing solutions to the problem at hand?" In other words, they combined knowledge, experience, and ingenuity. Not all became marketed products, but he developed them, nonetheless, to the last detail.

The telephone stand (U.S. Patent No. 1,371,747) allows a person to speak on the phone without holding the receiver to the ear. At the time, the most common domestic telephone was the candlestick variety, which held the transmitter on a "candlestick" post; the receiver was separate and held in the hand. When the phone was not in use, the receiver was hung on the fork of the switch hook (also attached to the stand), thus disconnecting the line. The candlestick phone had the convenience of proximity—you could place it near you on a table, desk, or other surface—and the inconvenience of limited mobility, since you had to hold the receiver during the entire conversation. This inconvenience was what Fischer sought to address.

"In using the telephone," he wrote in the specifications, "delays in making communications and details requiring attention during the conversation often necessitates [sic] the receiver being held to the ear for considerable periods. This is tedious and fatiguing. Arm rests and other devices of similar nature have been provided to mitigate the inconvenience, but there is not always space for such devices and in using them the two hands are not free."

The invention (shown in figure 8.1) consists of a base stand into which the telephone and receiver can be inserted, without use of any special brackets or tools. These stands hold two posts: a rigid one for the transmitter and a partly flexible one for the receiver; the latter can be bent into any position. A spring, attached to the clamp at the base of the transmitter, attaches at the other end to the telephone's switch, which itself is controlled by a spring. To receive a call, one only has to detach the spring from its hook and bring the mouth and ear close to the transmitter and receiver. Thus one can speak on the phone while using the hands for something else, such as writing or going through papers. The stand holds the telephone and receiver securely, yet the two can easily be removed for cleaning and repairs. [14]

The spring seems to play a minor role in this invention; it functions only as an easy means of releasing the switch. Yet this allows a person to take or end a call without moving the receiver; it is thus central to the phone stand's function. Moreover, the phone stand employs both rigidity and flexibility: rigidity of the base and the partial flexibility of the receiver post. Thus some of the concepts of the spring come into play even where no springs are involved.

The candlestick telephone would soon be rendered obsolete by Bell's model 102 telephone, which brought the transmitter and receiver into a single handpiece. In the meantime, Fischer's invention eliminated the inconvenience of having to hold the receiver while speaking. I can imagine him, prior to this invention, conducting business calls (maybe even about patents themselves) and gritting his teeth as he tried to flip through pages with one hand. Even while on the phone, he might have imagined alternatives.

Some of Fischer's inventions must have arisen out of conversations. Assuming he did not iron his own clothes—that was probably his wife's, Sadie's, job—he may have seen her wrestling with the cord, which continually got in the way of her work (since the cord plugged into a ceiling socket, the typical kind of socket at the time). Perhaps she complained about it over dinner. Maybe she proposed the idea: "Couldn't a spring be used to keep that cord out of the way?" The take-up spring was not an innovation in itself—such devices already existed—but this particular invention (U.S. Patent No. 1,578,817) brought several improvements. In particular, the two ends of the spring could be attached firmly to the cord at any two points (provided the distance between them was at least as great as the length of the device itself). One could adjust the spring without detaching the cord from the socket. The spring would expand and

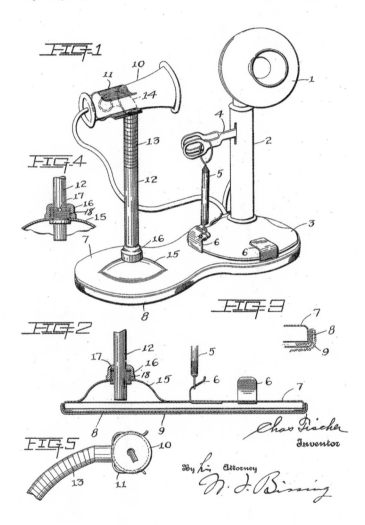

C. FISCHER.
TELEPHONE STAND.
APPLICATION FILED MAY 20, 1919.

1,371,747.                                                    Patented Mar. 15, 1921.

**Figure 8.1.    Charles Fischer (Inventor), Telephone Stand, U.S. Patent 1,371,747.**
*Fischer, Charles. 1921. Telephone stand. U.S. Patent 1,371,747, filed May 20, 1919, and issued March 15, 1921. The United States Patent and Trademark Office, http:// www.uspto.gov.*

retract in response to the force exerted on the cord; thus someone could iron without difficulty. The drawing is shown in figure 8.2.

In the patent specifications, Fischer described this spring's purpose:

My invention relates to take-up springs for electric cords used for electrical appliances, such as table lamps, electric irons and the like,

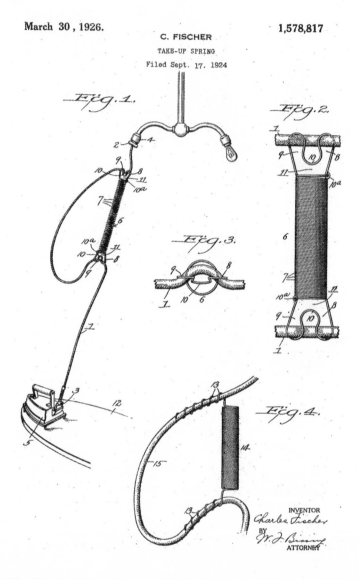

March 30 , 1926.                                                1,578,817

C. FISCHER

TAKE-UP SPRING

Filed Sept. 17, 1924

Figure 8.2.    Charles Fischer (Inventor), Take-Up Spring, U.S. Patent 1,578,817.
*Fischer, Charles. 1926. Take-up spring. U.S. Patent 1,578,817, filed September 17, 1924,
and issued March 30, 1926. The United States Patent and Trademark Office, http://
www.uspto.gov.*

and more particularly to a take-up spring which can be attached to the intermediate portion of a cord provided with connector plugs at the ends. The invention is especially useful in connection with taking up the cord of an electric iron, thus doing away with the inconvenience and annoyance of having the cord in the way of the iron when the latter is in use and permitting free use of the iron by the operator.[15]

Like the telephone stand, this device exists to eliminate a mundane and recurring problem. It may have come out of several intersecting, ongoing ponderings: about different things to do with springs, about ways of solving the problem at hand, and about ways of improving on existing solutions. While the take-up spring (like the telephone stand) seems eminently practical, both the drawings and description have beauty: "The cord is thus frictionally and yieldingly gripped by the ends of the spring so that the amount of slack of the cord to be taken up may be readily adjusted and the spring secured to any desired part thereof." I do not know whether anyone helped him with the writing, but it stands out for its precision and vigor.

To my knowledge, the most playful of Fischer's inventions was the book prop, a contraption that holds a book open and clamps gently but securely onto the leg, leaving your hands free while you read, draw, speak on the phone, or smoke. Initially named the Fischer Book-Prop and later branded the Cardinal Book-Prop, this gadget came in a whimsically designed box. Closely related to his earlier book stand, patented in 1922 (Patent No. 1,437,837), this device, manufactured in the 1930s, boasts a panoply of uses. (See figure 8.3.)

According to Charles Fischer's grandson Robert, this prop was a variation on map stands used by Navy pilots.[16] "The knee clamp concept in my Grandfather's Book Prop," Robert writes,

was explained to me as being derived from the bombardier equipment on those planes during actual missions. While he was scoping the bombing target, he needed a map to confirm the location. He placed the map in a flat easel resting on one knee, then "clamped" that easel on his knee so it could be a free-floating reference on the mission which permitted him incredible ease in pinpointing the target. Any number of maps could be laid on the easel at any time. It makes me smile to imagine some bombardier's grandmother, after the war, whipping up batches of chocolate chips using a bombing apparatus to hold her cookie recipe in place.

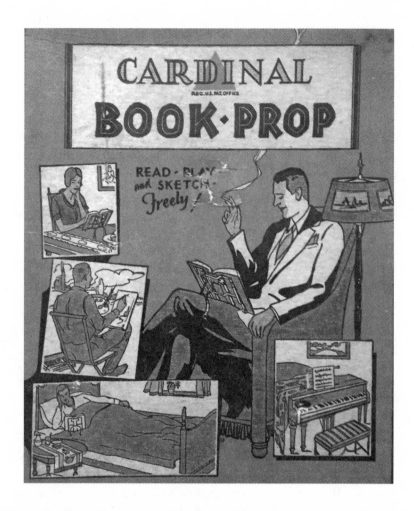

**Figure 8.3. Chas. Fischer Spring Co., Cardinal Book-Prop, Box Front.** *Photograph by Diana Senechal.*

Just as in Aristophanes' *Peace*, we see a wartime instrument adapted to times of peace; instead of holding a map on the knee for the sake of pinpointing the target, the prop-user may make cookies, paint a landscape, or gesticulate while reading. The device has two kinds of spring: two coil springs that hold the prop in its adjusted position and the knee clamp itself.

Despite their specific and specialized nature, these three inventions—telephone stand, take-up spring, and book prop—offer some clues to the nature of creativity. To create something new, one must be steeped in a

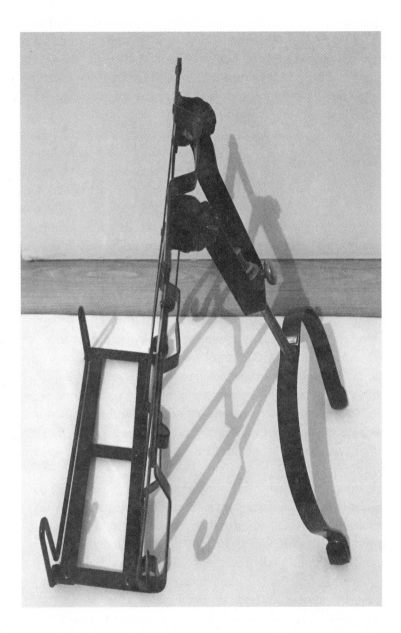

**Figure 8.4.    Chas. Fischer Spring Co., Cardinal Book-Prop.** *Photograph by Diana Senechal.*

subject; one advances within it by asking questions and improving on what has been done so far. Creativity involves learning from others;

Fischer must have done extensive research on existing patents and received advice on how to apply for new ones. He must have tested out his ideas not only alone but with others, listening to their reactions and suggestions. All of this seems relatively straightforward; why wail about a creativity crisis? Why not simply encourage students and others to tinker with their subjects?

Tinkering is one of the most difficult activities to encourage, since not everyone knows how to do it, and no two people do it in the same way. Nor is it always advisable; at early stages with a subject, it can lead to many dead ends. But a wise teacher can advise certain kinds of experimentation even early on. For example, when teaching musical technique, a teacher can recognize that the precise position of the hand may depend on the student's own proportions; instead of gripping the bow in one specific way, the student should find a rounded, relaxed grip that allows for flexibility of bowing.[17] In other words, the teacher can emphasize certain principles while giving the student room to work out details. As the student advances, she can figure out even more.

A teacher can also set an example and recognize students' unusual work. Teachers who work on problems independently, think about their subject, and pursue interesting hobbies will show all of this directly or indirectly; the students will recognize a mind at work. Those who draw attention to literary, artistic, and other works will influence their students, who, regardless of preferences, yearn to be exposed to new things. Likewise, those teachers who notice their students' wit and resourcefulness will make room for it in the school and beyond.

To encourage creativity, one must bring together knowledge and questioning. Some educators emphasize questioning, others knowledge, but neither has meaning without the other. There can be no generic approach to creativity; each discipline has its own principles, demands, and openings. Someone might show intense creativity in one field but not in another; some may find their way into creative work over many years.

An overt emphasis on creativity can discourage the creative act. Once, when assigning my students the task of writing a story, I made some time in the lesson for planning. One student told me that he did not write well among others, that his ideas came to him when he was alone. I recognized his point. Another student told me that his story did not meet the stated requirements; to meet them would require ruining the story, he thought. I read his story and realized that he was right. Any creative assignment can only help students get started, if it does that much. The assignment is often flawed, but if the teacher can see this, then the flaw can lead to good. Nor need all assignments be putatively creative in nature; creativity needs a break from the spotlight. Through learning about something, a student gathers material, structure, and ideas. All of these feed creativity without blasting its name. In contrast, a creativity workshop could end up dangling a set of clichés over a void.

One night in February 2018, I dreamt that I was teaching a drama class of fifty adult students of many ages (from twenties to seventies). Somehow I had been given the task of teaching them basic acting skills, without any specific content. I came up with an activity for them and assigned them to groups. We were outdoors in a large courtyard on a hill; I saw people disperse and heard voices grow louder. No one seemed to be listening to me; I realized, to my dismay, that I had nothing to say. An elderly couple started to head downhill; I asked them whether they would be taking part in the activity, and the wife said, with disdain, "I think not." Overwhelmed, I left the courtyard to gather my thoughts. I found myself downtown, perhaps in Budapest, trying to find my way back. I understood what had happened: the class had fallen apart because I was not teaching them anything. But now I myself was lost. I found my way back to the building; from there, someone pointed me to the classroom (no longer a courtyard). This strange dream made sense. To teach, you need to teach something; to act, you need working material.

Perhaps the worst thing for creativity is dogma. Dogma delights in nothing; it insists on its own rigid ways. To accomplish something meaningful, one can dig in to the problem at hand and learn about it slowly, sitting still for a while. Such learning, though sluggish at first, soon starts to wiggle with questions: "What does this mean?" "How does this work?" and "What if I did it this way?" This train becomes a way of life; ideas rumble in the stations, and then with a jolt and a ring they take off.

Let there be more creativity—in schools, workplaces, everywhere. In determining what this means, let us use imagination and knowledge; let us not fall into dull dicta about the needs of the workplace and century. The current economy does not hold a grip on our souls; it will soon change into something else, and that into something else. In the meantime, there are things worth doing that will still be worth doing tomorrow. Without beating poor creativity over the head, one can honor it gently, unassumingly, and daily. The take-up spring may no longer move earth and heaven or make ironing easier, but its principles remain. In our daily work, there are questions to answer, ideas to test out, and problems to solve; such tasks are worth a thousand cries for change.

# 9

# IN PRAISE OF MIXED MINDSETS

Why "Growth Mindset" May Not Always Be Ideal

In recent years, the concept of "growth mindset" has taken over schools and workplaces so rapidly that it must have a growth mindset of its own. Coined by the Stanford psychologist Carol Dweck, the term denotes an attitude toward intelligence and learning. A person with "growth mindset" believes that he or she can grow more intelligent, whereas someone with "fixed mindset" does not. In her extensive research, Dweck found that growth mindset, not innate ability, separates the achievers from the nonachievers; therefore, by cultivating a growth mindset, one increases one's possibilities. She acknowledges that people have a mixture of fixed and growth mindsets but maintains that people should strive for the latter. Thus the very concept of growth mindset contains an oversimplification; while grounded in careful, long-term research, it suffers from its own constrictions, even as it spreads far and wide.

Something akin to growth mindset makes sense; where would humanity be if it did not believe it could improve? How many people have held themselves back, needlessly, through excessive belief in their innate abilities (or lack thereof)? Some give up on math in elementary school, declaring, "I am not a math person"; others, long assured of their mathematical gifts, experience self-doubt, even despair, when struggling with calculus in college. Understanding that any serious endeavor takes work—and that people improve over time—allows us to set aside limiting notions and delve into the problem at hand.

Yet growth mindset represents only a partial truth. We contend daily with length and limitation, survival and mortality; to herald one over the other is to ignore part of our existence. Sometimes we must recognize our limits, sometimes not; sometimes we must charge ahead full steam, sometimes pause. There is nothing shameful or false in saying, at times, "I can't do this"; the admission can allow us to take a break or make room for other endeavors. Sometimes an ebb, halt, or diversion is in order; sometimes what matters is not our "growth" per se but our insight into a subject, even our hesitation around it.

My purpose here is not to dismiss Dweck's research but to show how the phrase "growth mindset" (which she previously called "incremental theory") interferes with investigation of the topic. [1] The phrase presumes, first of all, the existence of an overarching mindset and, second, the superiority of this particular one. Neither of these assumptions holds water (or vitamin juice). There is no reason to think that our attitudes are governed by a particular mindset or that growth mindset is desirable across the board. A mindset is different from a theory; while a theory is a coherent, logical, tentative explanation of observed phenomena, a mindset is an entire set of beliefs, an overarching attitude. Do we have an overarching attitude about ability, or do we have mixtures of experiences and beliefs? If we could cultivate a pure attitude of growth, would this improve our lives? Both questions remain open.

Mindset researchers routinely laud the growth mindset ideal. Mindset Works, an organization founded by Dweck, Lisa S. Blackwell, and Eduardo Briceño, offers, on its website, an eight-question "Mindset Assessment," through which visitors can discover which mindset they have. "The Mindset Assessment," the website explains, "is a quick diagnostic tool drawn from research-validated measures for people ages twelve and over to use to assess their mindsets. It has been used in many studies to show how mindsets can change, and can be used by you and your students to identify areas in which you can work toward a growth mindset." My own test results, according to the website, suggest that I have growth mindset but can still improve in some areas: "Even though you have a good foundation, there are some areas where you could benefit from learning how to cultivate your growth mindset practices." Why does the instrument assume that "fixed" and "growth" mindsets (and their combinations) are the only possibilities and that the more "growth mindset" we have, the better? Why does it not acknowledge any uncertainty?[2] To approach these questions, let us look at the theory's origins.

Dweck's theory of growth mindset grew out of her work on motivation, which began in the 1970s and took shape over time. In a landmark 1998 paper, she and Claudia M. Mueller discuss the outcomes of their research: They found that children praised for ability engaged less analytically with new tasks than children praised for effort. In addition, children praised for effort showed, on subsequent tasks, more motivation and persistence, fewer low-ability attributions ("I'm not good at this"), and higher performance than those praised for ability. Moreover, those praised for ability described intelligence as a fixed trait, whereas those praised for effort described it as malleable. From here, Dweck continued to shape her theories and test their applications. A 2015 study conducted by Dweck and colleagues suggests that even a brief online growth mindset intervention can lead to improved performance, especially by struggling students. Her 2006 book *Mindset*, along with her TEDx talk and popular articles, has influenced not only educators, students, and parents, but business executives, prodigies, and athletes.[3]

For the first of six studies described in the 1998 paper, Dweck and Mueller recruited a total of 128 fifth-graders from three schools: a midwestern public school and two public schools in a northeastern city. The students were given three sets of problems in sequence. After the first set, all participants, in both the experimental and control groups, were given positive feedback on their performance; regardless of their actual score, they were told that they did very well and solved a certain number constituting at least 80 percent of the problems. Those in the experimental group then received additional feedback: 41 were praised for their intelligence and 41 for their effort. Those in the control group received no additional feedback at all.

They then had to select one of the four options for their next performance or learning goal: "problems that aren't too hard, so I don't get many wrong"; "problems that are pretty easy, so I'll do well"; "problems that I'm pretty good at, so I can show I'm smart"; and "problems that I'll learn a lot from, even if I won't look so smart." After the second, difficult, set, they were all told that they had performed "a lot worse" and had solved only 50 percent of the problems. They were then asked to rate their task persistence, task enjoyment, and performance quality. They were also assessed for their attributions for poor performance on the second set of problems. For this, they had to assign weight to each of four statements; one of these expressed lack of effort, two lack of ability, and one lack of time. They were then instructed to assign weights to the importance of their smartness and hard work by coloring in portions of a circle.

The researchers found a significant correlation between type of praise and subsequent performance goal; those praised for intelligence tended to choose tasks that they thought would make them look smart, whereas those praised for effort tended to choose "problems that I'll learn a lot from, even if I won't look so smart." In addition, the researchers found differences among the groups in subsequent desire to persist, task enjoyment, and task performance. Those praised for intelligence reported less desire to persist and less task enjoyment than those in the effort and control groups (which did not differ significantly from each other on this measure), as well as more low-ability attributions. Also, those praised for intelligence showed a subsequent drop in performance, while those in the effort group showed improvement (and those in the control group, only slight improvement). The authors concluded that praise for effort predisposed these students to choose learning goals over performance goals, whereas praise for intelligence did the reverse. Praise for effort also had a positive effect on persistence, enjoyment, and performance, whereas praise for intelligence had a negative effect. The second through sixth studies expanded on, verified, and refined these findings.

While these findings seem promising, they also raise questions. To what extent were the students affected by the truth or falsity of the performance feedback? If, for instance, a participant solved the first set of problems confidently and correctly but was then told he solved 80 percent of them, would he not be confused and possibly lose trust in the experiment? Would he not especially distrust praise that focused on his intelligence? If I were a fifth-grader in this experiment, and if I found the first set easy, I might find it odd that I had gotten just 80 percent correct and therefore "must be smart at these problems." I might doubt the intelligence of the person calling me smart. Likewise, if I had solved only two or three of them correctly—and knew this—I might be puzzled by both the stated results and the praise. Praise for effort, in contrast, would not bring the same kind of confusion. Even if the reported score were inaccurate, I might think, "There's more to these problems than I realized." In other words, confounding factors may have interfered with the two types of praise and their effects. The subsequent studies discussed in the paper, while addressing certain potential problems, do not address those related to the content of the tests. The authors conclude, "Taken together, the findings from the six studies provide striking evidence for the differential effects that praise for intelligence and praise for hard work have on children's achievement behaviors and beliefs."[4] Thus, even here, the researchers may have overrelied on binary possibilities.

Binary characterizations of human nature and behavior can be catchy. The idea of praising effort (rather than intelligence) has hardened into slogan and chant; to Dweck's consternation, schools have equated such dogma with growth mindset itself. Growth mindset quotes adorn classroom walls; students perform growth mindset cheers. In training sessions, teachers and parents are warned against telling children that they are smart (or, presumably, that they have a talent). These pebbles of advice have avalanched into problems. A 2016 *Education Week* study of K–12 teachers found that teachers overwhelmingly supported the idea of growth mindset, that 80 percent were implementing what they perceived as growth mindset strategies in the classroom—in particular, praising students for effort and encouraging them to persist—but only 20 percent reported perceiving themselves as effective at this. Apparently posters, cheers, and word replacements were not doing the trick.[5]

Dweck has spoken out against these exaggerations and abuses, but they originate partly in the phrase "growth mindset" itself. Generic and sweeping, it seems to call for generic, sweeping application, which does not prove helpful. Which has more substance: praising students for effort or helping them tackle an actual problem? If a student is struggling to prove the Vertical Angles Theorem, for instance, does it do any good to say, "I see that you're trying hard. How wonderful for your brain!"? Or should the teacher instead hint, "Look at the supplementary angles and see whether that helps you"? If a student seems bewildered by passages in John Stuart Mill's *On Liberty*, the teacher can begin parsing them and then ask the student to complete the analysis. Such an approach not only encourages persistence but illuminates the topic.

The term "growth mindset" also encourages excessive focus on what the brain is doing. Besides encouraging navel-gazing—or, rather, neuron-gazing—this can lead parents and teachers to cite brain science that they do not understand. On NPR, Anya Kamenetz describes a professional development program in which teachers are "encouraged to praise students' efforts, ask them about another strategy they might try, or even talk directly about how hard their brains are stretching and growing." The big word of the day—"neuroplasticity"—gets taught in second-grade classrooms. Such brain talk is simplistic at best; the "growth" of the brain during learning may not be uniform or permanent.[6] Popularized brain science is prone to exaggeration and misinterpretation; teachers bringing it up in the classroom should exercise caution.

Brain science talk can not only mislead but distract from the matter at hand. When teaching *Hamlet*, I do not tell my students, "Your brains are growing right now as you figure out this text." Instead, we discuss the text. Yes, I help them see that they can come to understand it better than they did at first—but our focus is on lines like "Come, go we to the king: / This must be known; which, being kept close, might move / More grief to hide than hate to utter love" (2.1.114–116). Did my brain grow as I pondered this? Did my students' brains grow? To answer this question, I would need to be a neurologist with proper scanning equipment and the necessary knowledge for correct interpretation. Lacking these, I see good reason to focus on the play. On this matter, I believe Dweck would agree, at least in part.

In January 2017, in response to recent criticisms of mindset theory, research, and implementation, Dweck acknowledged areas of improvement, expressed gratitude for the criticism, and cited problems with existing growth mindset implementation. Growth mindset, she noted, was often poorly understood by parents and teachers; it should be treated not as a magic bullet or generic solution but as an approach whose success depended on "context and delivery." She pointed to papers in which she and her colleagues had identified and addressed problems with growth mindset practice: in particular, they cautioned against excessive blatancy and overemphasis on effort, calling instead for a combination of overt and "stealthy" methods and for more emphasis on helping students build a repertoire of approaches to their work.[7]

Yet while acknowledging some errors in research and implementation, Dweck affirms the overall soundness of mindset theory. While acknowledging that we all have mixtures of growth and fixed mindsets, she sees pure growth mindset as the ultimate goal. This cannot be faked, she emphasizes; by "banning" fixed mindset, we may actually blind ourselves to its presence in us and create "false growth mindsets" that will defeat true growth mindset's purpose. "If we watch carefully for our fixed-mindset triggers," she writes, "we can begin the true journey to a growth mindset." That is, to move toward growth mindset, we need keen self-awareness, not a set of feel-good slogans.[8] This makes eminent sense but still misses part of the problem.

There is no reason to accept a growth mindset as an absolute ideal. Let us consider in detail how a mixed mindset may have more to offer—and may more closely characterize a working mind—than a growth mindset alone.

Pure growth mindset, in all areas of life, would be exhausting; one needs the liberty to make selections, acknowledge limitations, and take breaks. Moreover, any serious endeavor takes shape as it goes along; to participate in this shaping, one must select certain options (within the endeavor) and discard others, thus employing a mixture of mindsets as well as good judgment. Also, any mindset benefits from its counterparts; a single mindset of any kind would constrict us, but contrasting mindsets open up possibilities. The mind is not even "set," for that matter; it continually creates new models, even for its own learning.

What causes a person to give up a pursuit? Many reasons and motives besides defeatism come into play. Sometimes a particular challenge is entirely optional and brings continual agony. Consider the bagpipe student who not only dreads practicing and recitals but drives her family crazy with the flailing, sputtering tones. Suppose she has no particular reason to learn the bagpipes and finds herself much more drawn to the ukulele. She may decide to quit the one and devote herself to the other; is there shame in this? Most of us have quit something so that we could focus on something else; unless we become serial quitters, or unless our choices aggrieve others, no one faults us for making a selection. Ethan *could* have improved at glass-blowing but opted for fencing instead.

Sometimes a fixed mindset is actually well founded. Some activities and pursuits demand abilities that we lack; people are not equally gifted in all areas. Not everyone has the flexibility to be a gymnast or the agility to be a basketball player; not everyone can excel at improv comedy. Anyone can enjoy these activities at an amateur level, but some may find the very amateurishness distressing. People can improve, sometimes considerably, in activities that they find difficult, but must they do so? Is it not liberating to leave the clumsiness behind? A fixed mindset—the acknowledgment that one is not good at certain things—can open up promise and possibility. No longer obsessed with trying to inch closer to a split (in gymnastics), I can instead pursue long-distance running or rowing. There is no shame in relative ease.

Sometimes a pursuit demands resources that exceed what we have or wish to spend. A professional tennis player at the low end of the rankings must participate, at her own expense, in as many tournaments as possible, just to make a living and stay in the game. The seemingly glamorous life of tennis players exists only at the top, and then with many strains; others may face continual financial and logistical struggle. A good tennis player could reasonably decide that this is too much, that she would rather pursue stable employment or return to school. To make this shift, she needs both growth mindset and fixed mindset (and much more): the ability to see and pursue possibilities outside of tennis, the ability to give up professional tennis, and the equanimity and self-knowledge for this simultaneous pursuit and relinquishment.

Sometimes an extended pursuit brings distress to the self and others, particularly in the area of romance. Dweck states that in relationships, one can have a fixed mindset in three ways: "You can believe that *your* qualities are fixed, your *partner's* qualities are fixed, and the *relationship's* qualities are fixed—that it's inherently good or bad, meant-to-be or not meant-to-be. . . . The growth mindset says all of these things can be developed." Yet sometimes a growth mindset proves unhelpful. Suppose you have been attracted to someone for years and believed that a relationship *could* form. The other person either does not reciprocate your interest or is not in a position to do so—yet with your growth mindset, you believe in the slightest hints of possibility. Your growth mindset, in this instance, can easily become obsessive, obnoxious, and intrusive; it is kinder to let the person go and direct your attention elsewhere. Dweck does acknowledge that both members of a relationship have to be willing to work on it—but they must also have the courage to say "enough." A combination of mindsets—giving up here but persisting with relationships generally—can save the day, even a life.[9]

Our mortality—not only our limited life span but our limited energy from day to day—compels us to select our pursuits carefully. We are not perpetual motion machines; some doors, including our own minds, swing shut at times. Each day we come up against tiredness and sleep. Given our limited time, and given the benefits of not rushing around frantically, aren't we better off selecting a few things to do, especially in adulthood, when our responsibilities and projects become more complex? Selection allows for tranquility. The selections need not be fatalistic or rigid; a person who quit the chess club the previous year might want to join again. A college student might take a class in number theory after deciding to major in architecture. Making selections does not mean giving up curiosity and playfulness. But there should be no shame or disaster in allowing the day, year, or life to have its limits.

A temporary fixed mindset—"This is all I can do today" or "I am resting today"—allows for sleep and renewal. This can be especially difficult with intellectual work, where ideas may come to mind on any day and at any hour. How do you halt when a poem has just started in your head, when you have an inkling how to solve a math problem, or when you see the direction your essay should take? One might feel compelled to seize an idea whenever it comes to mind, but there are benefits to holding back. First, the idea does not go away; the mind does not forget it so easily and may even take care to remember it. Second, a day of total rest can invigorate the mind and body; the subsequent ideas and work may be better, not worse. Third, such rest allows us to keep ourselves and our work in perspective; the world does not depend entirely on us, nor we entirely on others. Finally, such rest allows for contemplation. Thus a temporary fixed mindset—a willingness to stop striving for a little while—can open up into thought.

Even discouragement—fixed mindset with a vengeance—can play a role in a larger endeavor. If, after a failed audition, I shut the door and do not emerge for several days, others may conclude that I have given up, that I am being "too hard on myself," or that I have succumbed to fixed mindset, the greatest of all ills. In fact, such withdrawal may give me room for introspection; I may need some time away from others' reassurance and advice. On my own, I can assess what went wrong and where I want to go from here. Perhaps I will keep on auditioning; perhaps I will step back to work on my skills.

A fixed mindset can help not only with choices among projects but with a project's structure and direction. When working on something substantial, such as a book or film, we often have to change course slightly (or drastically), discarding one idea for something better. An untrammeled growth mindset would make that impossible; we would insist on refining and revising that first idea, even if it clearly didn't work. A fixed mindset, in this case, allows us to admit that a particular idea or approach has not worked. That refreshes the project and allows it to take new form.

Growth mindset and fixed mindset (and other mindsets) work best in combination—not only because our lives call for such mixtures but because any mindset on its own has inherent limitations and fails to represent humanity. The person who believes exclusively in progress (his own, other people's, and that of society) may ridicule expressions of suffering; the one who believes in failure may likewise ridicule hope. Only through a complex combination of mindsets can one avoid self-satisfaction and dogmatism. A person needs more than one way of viewing the world, since truth often transcends our everyday categories. Progress and lack of progress, success and failure take part in something larger. To glimpse it, sometimes we need a mix and clash of views.

These considerations lead to the question: Are "growth mindset" and "fixed mindset" the most helpful terms? Are our choices dictated by our mindset, or are they more often influenced by our judgment, priorities, virtues, vices, morals, aesthetic sense, interests, feelings, and duties? If so, the question becomes not how to develop growth mindset but how to develop knowledge itself, along with discipline and discernment. The mind continually revises its models; as we learn and work on things, our perception of learning changes subtly. We start to see the structures of what we do—and within them, liberties and openings, many of these changing, many remaining fixed, as we move through work and thought.

Do we have the discipline to persist with things when we should and to give them up when that is best? Do we have the discernment to distinguish between the two situations and all the subtleties within them? Few of us have discipline and discernment across the board; how do we develop and sustain these qualities in relation to subject matter?

Discipline begins in elementary school (or earlier), when we start studying subjects we have not ourselves chosen and do not necessarily like. At this age, students cannot opt out of mathematics, English, or other subjects; they must participate in class and learn the fundamentals. In the best curricula, these basic skills combine with lively subject matter; students learn not only persistence, not only skills, but interesting things. As Dweck herself has noted, teachers, instead of preaching growth mindset, can help students see *how* they can tackle challenges, improve, and grow as individuals in the process. Students who complain, "I'm no good at math" can learn how to identify their primary area of difficulty, make progress within it, and gain insight. Those who find math easy can take their learning to higher levels; the teachers and schools should find ways to keep them challenged, whether through advanced classes, special tutorials and projects, or math clubs and competitions.

During the elementary years, children may also take up an instrument, participate in a play, or develop a particular athletic skill; while those activities are optional, parents and teachers can help them resist initial urges to quit. The degree of persistence will depend on the child's wishes and the judgment of teacher and parent; in the best scenario, the child can see some of the rewards of persistence and decide, over time, what to make of them.

In secondary school, students start to choose electives and extracurricular activities. If they have already developed a disciplined approach to study, they will take difficulty in stride and figure out ways to overcome it. Even so, they may be tempted to pursue subjects that they immediately like, that seem useful to them, or that draw on their known abilities. While none of this is wrong, teachers can encourage them to seek a counterbalance: to test and extend themselves with subjects that they find irrelevant or intimidating. A student who has trouble remembering historical facts—and who therefore has lost interest in history—may rekindle an interest when reading historical interpretations and primary source documents. Someone who finds physics dull may suddenly take to electricity and magnetism. These early fascinations may stay with the student and inspire future studies. So even as students gravitate toward their personal interests, they benefit from continued encouragement and demands.

In college, students have some liberty to select courses; they must choose and fulfill a major, but beyond that, and beyond other distributional requirements and core curricula, they may choose from a range of courses across the subjects and participate in campus cultural life (literary magazines, musical and theatrical groups, political groups, athletic teams, special events and lectures, and so forth). Their ability to make the most of this liberty will depend on their preparation and intention. Some may take off in unexpected directions; others will stick closely to their initial career goals. Still others will strike a combination of conservatism and daring, of practicality and play.

Beyond college, in workplaces, young adults will encounter pressure to demonstrate a career trajectory—that is, to show that they are continually striving toward advancement. Perhaps this is not true for them; perhaps they see their job as a way to make a living so that they can do other things in their free time. That is, they may be advancing, but not on other people's terms. With a complex view of the world, such people can defend their own choices; they know that their most important endeavors may be unknown and unseen by others, at least for an interval. Fixed and growth mindsets may appear in each other's costumes; someone who appears stagnant may be striving and improving in private, while a go-getter may stick to the formula.

All this said, the work of Dweck and her colleagues has drawn attention to a vital issue and idea. Throughout our lives, we learn and improve; when we understand how to do so, we improve even more. Not only Dweck's research but a large body of scholarship and experience points to the malleability of intelligence. [10] This is especially important to those who have historically been treated as less intelligent than others and who have come to see themselves similarly. The old practices of separating people by supposed innate ability—of testing for IQ or talent, praising students for their intelligence, or creating programs for gifted kindergarteners—rest on misconceptions and can do great damage. To help students and others find their capacity for growth is to work with possibility. Dweck's work has helped people discover what they could do—at school, at work, in the world, in their private lives, and in their thoughts.

Yet one can do this while grappling with truth in its complexity. The problem with "growth mindset" is not the idea of improvement but the assumptions inherent in the phrase. Mindset research would grow in import if it both recognized and honored a mixture. We are limited and unbounded: capable of more than we realize but also incapable of doing everything, and mortal on top of it all. Our limitations, subtle and blatant, conditional and absolute, are part of our striving. Social sciences have much to learn from literature; works from *The Epic of Gilgamesh* to Homer's *Iliad* to Shakespeare's *The Tempest* to Jorge Luis Borges's "The Garden of Forking Paths" probe humans' finiteness and infinity.

These works suggest far more than growth, far more than limitation. Literature takes us out of our regular categories, our usual sounding of words. In literature, we find ourselves at least slightly wrong; there is something more, something tilted, a great unsettling of what we have known until now. There is no reason to submit to a slogan—"growth mindset" or any other—when allowed such a library and life.

# 10

# WHAT DO WE MEAN BY "WE"?

We live in a time of pronoun profusion. Schools, workplaces, and other institutions have recognized and instituted pronouns beyond "he" and "she" (such as ey, s/he, ze, xe, ve, and e); their official forms now provide a fillable blank for gender. Many colleges now recommend asking people which pronoun they wish to use. Through honoring others' pronouns, the argument runs, we also honor their identity.[1] Some welcome these changes; others resist them. But in all this tumult, another pronoun—the first-person plural "we"—has sidestepped the red tape and continues to cause mischief of its own. It even made its way into the first sentence of this essay.

"We" speaks for a group that may not even exist: "we believe," "we need," and other phrases often spin a collective out of thin air. Such is the mischief of "we": it professes unity and agreement, often without cause. But we could not live without "we," even in its vaguer shades; through it, we articulate common purpose, without which a country or individual cannot survive. Even the most literal "we" articulates a myth; such myth can deceive or enlighten both the individual and the group. I have set out here to investigate the myths of "we" and their effects on intellectual life.

"We" has an uneasy place in language. Over the centuries and across languages and cultures, people have used alternatives to it, perhaps because of its slipperiness. Yet these alternatives work poorly in English. In Russian, the pronoun is often not needed at all; thus one can say *poni-maem*, "we understand." Russian also uses passive constructions to indicate a general understanding; *razumeetsia* (literally, "it is understood") has the approximate colloquial meaning of "of course." English cannot dispense with pronouns so easily, and its passive constructions risk convolution. German and its relatives often use "man," roughly translated as "people" or "one"; in English, "one" can sound stilted and awkward. In informal English, it is common to use "you" or "people" ("they") to refer to humans in general; both have the drawback that they do not include the speaker and can thus sound distant or patronizing.

Consider the differences between the following statements (intended to refer to humans in general):

> We cannot live without longings; even impossible wishes pull us forward.
> One cannot live without longings; even impossible wishes pull one forward.
> You cannot live without longings; even impossible wishes pull you forward.
> People cannot live without longings; even impossible wishes pull them forward.
> A person cannot live without longings; even impossible wishes pull him or her forward.
> A man cannot live without longings; even impossible wishes pull him forward.

Of these variations, the "we" is clearest and most elegant. "One" and "a person" suffer from cumbersomeness, "you" seems slightly accusatory or haughty, "people" requires a continued use of third-person plural (which will soon become awkward through the repetitions of "they"), and "a man" seems to exclude women. Thus "we," in this instance, seems preferable to its alternatives. Yet it provokes objections; immediately someone may respond, "Who is the 'we' here? This does not apply to me." It takes just one exception to deflate a "we" on the spot.

Some try to avoid the errors of "we" by speaking only in the first-person singular. Who can assail or even question that? Yet such an approach leads to insularity; if I may speak only of my own experience, and if my own experience is immune to questioning or criticism from others, then there is nothing to discuss at all. People speak of themselves and retreat into silence: "It's my opinion; you are welcome to your own," or "It's my story; I get to tell it in my own way." Opinion and narration no longer need defense, since they begin with and return to the self.

As for "we," its cup of fiction overflows; that is both its price and its gift. Even when used in its most literal, direct sense—to indicate a specific plurality, such as two specific people—"we" necessarily invents a scenario, since the person uttering the word speaks for someone else (and can never be fully qualified to do so). Consider this imaginary yet recognizable family exchange:

**Jane:** So can I be in the musical?

**Lisa:** Your father and I discussed this last night, and we think it's fine, as long as you promise to keep up with your homework.

**Robert:** I never agreed to any such thing.

**Lisa:** But wasn't that what we decided?

**Robert:** I said I'd think about it.

Here Lisa imagines an agreement that does not exist; this fiction takes the form of "we." Even if she had not misinterpreted Robert's words, her "we" would distill a process of discussion, disagreement, thinking, deliberation, and final consensus. Even at its most precise, "we" stands for something more complex.

What if those included in the "we" have agreed beforehand—for instance, in a petition—to take part in it? Signatories are no guarantee of precision; someone can sign a petition without agreeing with all of its points (or even reading it carefully). Some people may have signed reluctantly or provisionally; some who supported the petition's statement might have refrained from signing, perhaps because they distrusted the organizers or because they do not sign petitions at all. Thus even here, where "we" refers to specific, identified names, it denotes an imagined unity. The question then becomes: Where lies the good, and where the harm, of such fiction?

I have puzzled over "we" for years. When making final revisions to my first book, *Republic of Noise*, I kept knocking into the word. Was it warranted in a book about solitude? How could I claim to call for an independent life of the mind while also speaking about a plural experience? I decided to address this issue (without resolving it) in the introduction.

> When I use "we" to describe a cultural tendency, I recognize that there
> are many outliers. Personal observations, psychological and sociologi-
> cal studies, and historical and literary works help define this "we"—
> but how can I claim to be part of this group when, by virtue of writing
> about it, I stand outside it? I answer that I am part of this "we" even as
> I view it from the outside.

This passage does not ring with conviction, yet its uncertainty is the
point. Is there a viable "we" that applies to contemporary culture? Is there
anything that we need, want, know, assume, remember, treasure, and
seek? Or is it up to each individual to find meaning? A forced "we" can
flatten and constrict experience, while the absence of "we" can lead to
personalized mayhem, a showdown of Twitter rants, and an erratic worldview. To handle "we" properly, a culture must grapple intelligently with
its own myths; it must understand those elements that bring people together, even imperfectly.

The manipulations of "we" have all the trappings, but none of the
depth, of myth. When using "we" to promote a political or business
agenda, a speaker assumes moral high ground, presumes to know what
others want, or subordinates individual differences to an external goal.
The "we" serves a narrow end, not a broad one. For example, when a
company spokesperson says, "We cannot afford to let our competitors get
ahead of us," the "we" does not refer to the collection of individuals
present. Possibly everyone included in the "we" will be fine. Rather,
"we" refers to the company itself; the individuals merely serve the company's interests. If "we" cannot afford to let the competitor get ahead,
then "we" must work long and hard to prevent this from happening. There
is nothing transcendent here, just a push for longer work hours or similar
measures.

In manipulative rhetoric, "we" serves the agenda of a group (or its
leadership) while ignoring or downplaying the views of the individual
members. Both the political right and the political left exploit this kind of
"we."

In his *Politics by Other Means: Higher Education and Group Thinking* (1992), David Bromwich questions the conservative George Will's
use of the phrase "we need," in *Statecraft as Soulcraft*, which argues that
a government should actively mold its citizenry through curriculum and
other initiatives:

> We need, says Will, a literature of cheerful sociability; and from each according to his ability, to each—but let us stop a moment at the phrase "we need." . . . It is a phrase most commonly heard at the end of committee reports and academic reviews. And it is a nuisance. To begin with, it does not identify the "we" who need. . . . The truth is, all that we, as participants in a culture, need at any time, and all we can intelligibly ask for, are interested descriptions of our way of life, which set us thinking about how it might be strengthened and how it might be reformed. By contrast, the topos of "we" always has an effect of bullying.[2]

Bromwich objects, in this context, specifically to the "topos" of "we"—that is, the axioms and argument it implies. The phrase "we need" presumes, first, that there is such a "we"; second, that everyone in this group needs the same thing; and third, that the speaker knows what this is. Each of these assumptions should be questioned.

Later in the book, Bromwich shines the light on professionalized academia, which likewise uses "we" for its own purposes:

> As with the conformists of the civilization, so with the conformists of the profession, the voice to distrust is the "we"-voice of collective judgment. . . . Recall the professionalist maxim: "We need to teach not the texts themselves but how we situate ourselves in reference to those texts." How many *we*'s are here! In a mood of such bureaucratized narcissism, it has become necessary to assert the obvious: we do not even know who we are, except in the long run.[3]

Here, too, the problem lies not in the practice of reading texts together, but in the idea that "we" (or anyone, for that matter) should focus on "how we situate ourselves in reference to those texts," as though such "situating" were possible, teachable, or subject to generalization.

Bromwich shows that in both cases—of conservative culture guards and academic trend enforcers—"we" takes on a domineering, arrogant aspect; this "we" does not exist except as a means of enforcing a particular dogma. The people using the pronoun do not take the time to define its contours; instead, they claim to speak for all. This "we" invites no dialogue; it stares into the crowd, nodding as though to say, "Now that we've established these facts, let's move on."

Such "we"-talk is par for the course in mission statements, commencement speeches, policy platforms, policy updates, and other lofty places. A manipulative "we" is often recognizable through its equivocation: in one sentence it means one thing, and in the next, another. On July 25, 2017, at a rally in Youngstown, Ohio, President Donald Trump used "we" in at least three ways, referring to himself, those present, and a vague American public.[4] Near the beginning, he states, "On Saturday I was in Virginia with thousands of brave men and women of the United States Military. Do we love the United States military? We commissioned the newest, largest, and most advanced aircraft carrier in the history of our nation, the USS *Gerald R. Ford* into the great American fleet." Here both occurrences of "we" sound vaguely royal; it was Trump himself who commissioned the supercarrier. A little later, he continues in this royal vein: "We have spent the entire week celebrating with the hard working men and women who are helping us make America great again. I'm here this evening to cut through the fake news filter and to speak straight to the American people." So far, "we" and "I" appear interchangeable.

A little further along, the meaning of "we" shifts. First comes a pronoun storm, where "their," "you," "its," and "we" occur in close succession. "Everyone in this arena is united by their love, and you know that. Do we know that. Everyone. United by their love for this country and their loyalty to one another, their loyalty to its people. [*Cheers*] And we want people to come into our country who can love us and cherish us and be proud of America and the American flag." After enumerating various things in which the crowd supposedly believes, he hits the peak of this particular segment: "We believe in freedom, self-government, and individual rights. We cherish and defend—thank you, it looks like it's in very good shape—our Second Amendment." The crowd cheers, and the "we" has done its job, purporting to represent the people there.

Then comes a third "we," which refers to a more general populace, not just those present. Trump achieves this through a sleight of words. "And finally," he says, "we believe that family and faith, not government and bureaucracy, are the foundation of our society. You've heard me say it before on the campaign trail and I'll say it again tonight. In America we don't worship government. We worship God." The "we" has morphed under the listeners' ears; now it refers to a true American, who, according to Trump, believes in "family and faith" as the foundation of American society. A true American worships God, not government (although Trump himself devoted some resources to attaining presidential power). The false dilemma—why should anyone have to choose between God and government?—merges with false generalization. "We" dissolves into a pious muddle, an American puddle.

For sure, one does not have to be Donald Trump to misuse "we." Democratic presidential candidate Hillary Clinton spread the "we's" liberally onto her speeches—for instance, at the Ohio Democratic Party Legacy Dinner in March 2016.[5] After detailing some of Trump's abuses on the campaign trail, she claimed unity with her audience. "Now you and I know," she said, "Donald Trump is not who we are. Now of course we can criticize and protest Mr. Trump all we want. But none of that matters if we don't also show up at the polls. If you want to shut him down, then let's vote him down, and then let's raise up a better future for ourselves and our children." All of this seems innocuous—a simple plea to turn up at the polls—except for the first "we" of the quote. At one level it's a truism that "Donald Trump is not who we are" (only Trump can be Trump); at another, it's a possible falsehood, since the "we" of America has many divisions. If "we" refers to Democrats alone, then the question still remains how "we" will "raise up a better future for ourselves and our children," since this will presumably require consensus with Republicans and others. In other words, Clinton's "we" vacillates between the specific and the general.

Such vacillation of "we" is par for the course in political speeches, but it appears in other contexts as well. Many of us have, at some point, used "we" to refer to other people, the general public, or the crowd. Without censoring such use of "we," one can examine and question it. Discussing the public's bias in favor of extroverted leaders, Susan Cain writes, "Culturally, we tend to associate leadership with extroversion and attach less importance to judgment, vision and mettle. We prize leaders who are eager talkers over those who have something to say. In 2004, we praised George W. Bush because we wanted to drink a beer with him. Now we criticize President Obama because he won't drink one with us." Evidently she does not include herself in this "we"—she criticizes this very tendency—yet, by using "we," she signals that she is one of the crowd. This results in ambiguity: Who, indeed, is this "we"? Who would choose to have a beer with Bush rather than Obama? Who has criticized Obama for not having a beer with him or her? (Obama is not averse to having beer with others; in 2009 he famously invited Henry Louis Gates Jr. and Sgt. James Crowley, who had arrested Gates at his own home, to the White House for a "beer summit.") Granted, Cain refers to "beer" symbolically, not literally; even so, many individuals fall outside her "we." This affects the larger argument, which relies on generalizations, not only of "us" but also of personality types. Bill Clinton—one of Cain's examples of blatant extroversion—has described himself as an introvert; Obama's describers disagree over his type. I wonder why presidents—and people in general—have to be classified as introverts or extroverts in the first place. More than one "we" in the article—or a combination of "we" and "they"—breaks down upon inspection.[6]

The pronoun "we" and its accomplices can serve as tools for scolding. In a draft version of an opinion piece for the Association for Psychological Science's *Observer* magazine, Susan Fiske, a social psychologist at Princeton and the former head of the APS, wrote about the current state of "methodological terrorism," in which, according to Fiske, researchers were being bullied, vilified, and sometimes even destroyed online by critics. The piece—which met with both praise and rebuke and which Fiske later modified—concludes (in both the draft and final versions):

> Ultimately, science is a community, and we are in it together. We agree to abide by scientific standards, ethical norms, and mutual respect. We trust but verify, and science improves in the process. Psychological science has achieved much through collaboration, but also through responding to constructive adversaries who make their critiques respectfully. The key word here is constructive.[7]

But is science a community, and who is the "we" who are "in it together"? A commenter on Andrew Gelman's blog pointed out that "science is *not* a community; it's a method." Moreover, "communities do not generally value the truth over their members' well-being (in either the material or emotional sense)." If science is a community, then by Fiske's logic, its members have no business criticizing each other freely and openly, since that would violate community spirit.[8] To say that "we are in it together" means that we have some responsibility to support and protect each other, rather than to point out errors and pursue greater accuracy. While Fiske rightly objects to online viciousness and name-calling, her "community" metaphor fits the situation poorly, since scientific inquiry involves sharp disagreements, open questioning, and unfettered critique.

"We" is the pundit's favorite pronoun; it conveys authority and importance. David Brooks uses "we" liberally, sometimes with justification, sometimes not. In a trenchant piece on the imperilment of democracy, he writes, "In short, we used to have a certain framework of decency within which we held our debates, and somehow we've lost our framework. We took our liberal democratic values for granted for so long, we've forgotten how to defend them. We have become democrats by habit and no longer defend our system with a fervent faith." He then promises, over the coming months, "to use this column, from time to time, to go back to first principles, to go over the canon of liberal democracy—the thinkers who explained our system and why it is great."[9] His words ring true, but who is the "we"? In offering to "go back to first principles," he suggests that he himself has not forgotten what they are. Perhaps out of politeness he includes himself within the "we" who "lost our framework," but he then makes clear that he stands outside the group. The "we" thus takes on a slightly patronizing tone, even if his overall message conveys humility.

One can find many more examples of a slippery "we" in politics, science, literature, education, and elsewhere—I cringe when I see it in my own work—but what is to be done about it? How can people keep the pronoun while guarding against its manipulations? One solution would be to create additional pronouns for the first-person plural. Yet this would only lead to rigidity and confusion; sometimes a "we" *must* refer to more than one plurality.

Another solution would be to state in advance what "we" means and to what it refers. While honorable, such clarity could easily become cumbersome. People using "we" in the simplest ways would have to stop, define their terms, and then slowly proceed, losing some of their audience in the meantime. Poems with "we" would get bogged down in footnotes. High school essays would dally in their first drafts, as students read and reread their teachers' comments: "Please explain and justify each use of 'we.'" This would not do: a pronoun is meant as a shortcut, not a detour; it offers ease, not burdens.

One could get rid of "we" altogether, but that would not work for long; we need "we" as much as we need anything. A we without "we" goes poor, bare, and forked; not knowing what to call itself, it pokes haplessly at the alphabet, scraping a letter here and there but peeling off no meaning. There must be room for a "we" of the imagination, a "we" that stretches beyond definitions without encroaching on liberty.

Such a common plurality presupposes myth: a legend or idea that comes out of memory and imagination combined. Dennis Patrick Slattery describes myth as memory and imagination; without one or the other, the myth would deteriorate. "History without the force of the poetic imagination working on it dissolves into facts and numbers; poetic imagination without history degenerates into fancy." Imagination itself is no trivial matter; in the words of Gaston Bachelard, "Imagination is not, as its etymology would suggest, the faculty of forming images of reality; it is rather the faculty of forming images which go beyond reality, which *sing* reality. It is a superhuman faculty."[10] To understand such myth, one must know its stories, history, questions, allusions, and resonances; one must hear its song.

The Declaration of Independence envelops such myth. The famous words, "We hold these truths to be self-evident, that all men are created equal, that they are endowed by their Creator with certain unalienable Rights, that among these are Life, Liberty and the pursuit of Happiness," have come to include, with each generation, a wider and deeper "we." To understand these words, one must know their history, sources, debates, and resonances. Are they to be interpreted literally, or is there a different way of hearing them? What does it mean to be "created equal" and to have "unalienable Rights"? What is the "pursuit of Happiness"? By looking into these questions, we increase our understanding and, with that, our commonality. So, too, with other texts that employ a general "we"; through reading and rereading them, through coming to understand their nuances, each individual can participate in the "we" without blindly acceding to it.

Robert Frost's poetry abounds with the mythical "we"—which he invokes subtly and cunningly, often bringing out a corresponding solitude and separation. In his sonnet "The Oven Bird," the bird is immediately presented as mythological: "There is a singer everyone has heard, / Loud, a mid-summer and a mid-wood bird / Who makes the solid tree trunks sound again." The reader is called upon to remember it (What bird is this? When have I heard it?) while listening, through the poem, to its song. (John Hollander remarks, "Come now, people in London have no more heard that singer than a New Englander would hear a nightingale.") From here, the "we" disappears from sight until the poem's turn or pause: "And comes that other fall we name the fall." The myth now encompasses both hearing and naming; we are brought into creation itself and, with that, into loss, into the poem's final question that the oven bird "frames in all but words." Puzzles fill the poem; we must consider what it means that the bird "knows in singing not to sing." Does the bird, as Hollander suggests, know to resist being allegorized? Does it stand, then, against the "we" that diminishes things, the "we" that comforts itself with clichés? If so, the poem raises up one "we" against another, almost invisibly. [11]

A mythical "we"—that is, a "we" that refers to an imaginary yet essential plurality—requires imagination, knowledge, and solitude. At its best, the "we" of a country, school, or institution does not force consensus but instead allows for a range of informed opinions, a range of ways of thinking about the world. Thus a mythical "we" relies on education.

What kind of education supports the mythical "we"? First of all, it must be steeped in language and literature. It must also emphasize history: not only its events but also its writings, scientific discoveries, and artistic works. In addition, throughout the grades, it should include a progression and careful selection of mathematics, sciences, and arts, so that students learn different ways of thinking, reasoning, investigating, and creating. Through these studies, students develop a complex understanding of individuals and culture; they learn how countries have come together and apart; they see the relationships between solitude and community. Such understandings allow for a profound "we" that consists not of fabricated unity but of true common experience and understanding.

If this seems like a lot of work for one pronoun, consider how much more the pronoun "I" demands. Self-knowledge requires more than communal knowledge; to know who you are, you must be capable not only of introspection but of continual striving within specific disciplines and tasks. I know myself as I prepare a Torah portion, revise a passage in this book, bike along the Zagyva river, write to a friend, or prepare for teaching. The self exists in motion, and its motion is unique; no one on the outside can direct it. To learn to guide oneself, one must learn and break from guides. The "I" listens closely to others and to itself but ultimately takes its own course; in doing so, it adds to the teachings of the world.

Yet there is a pronoun still more difficult than "I": the steep and dazzling "you," unteachable and only rarely known. The "you" comes to us only in flashes—when we are reading a story, speaking with a friend, or maybe biking through the countryside. In this moment, we face someone or something outside the self; it comes to us not packaged, but packageless and boundless, beyond anything we can name or describe. Martin Buber writes of the aloneness of this encounter; you cannot speak about it to others, but it can teach you "to meet others, and to hold your ground when you meet them."[12] The greatest and most elusive of guides, this "you" comes and vanishes without warning and cannot be condensed into maxims. To learn the "you," one must accept the uncertainties of life; one must seek not to define or possess others but to tolerate empty-handed-ness. This "you" permeates religion but does not require religion; it can be glimpsed in secular studies, work, and brief conversations with strangers. The everyday "you" has little to do with this encounter; when we say "you," we usually mean something limited, some mixture of expectation, fulfillment, and disappointment. If I ask, "What are you doing this weekend?" I expect a summary; the "you" here is compact, not expansive. Out of courtesy and expediency, we compress our "I's" and "you's"; we summarize ourselves and expect summaries. Yet the true "you" cannot be summarized at all.

Back to the "we": no matter how we understand and handle it, it poses difficulty. To reckon with the pronoun, we must face this difficulty, staying alert to platitudes and manipulations. The concept of "we" can fuel a cult or inspire a civilization; it can shut people out or invite them in. Learning these distinctions, we can say "we" with intention and conscience; when hearing it, we can join it or not, as we choose. In this way, we can think for ourselves while learning from others' work and lives. The motto *e pluribus unum* suggests a joining of plural and singular, not in confusion but in clarity and honor. This unity is never finally found— we find and lose it throughout our lives—but in chasing and gathering the strands, we continue a worthy project.

# 11

# A GOOD MISFIT

How Mismatches Can Enrich Our Work and Life

In schools, workplaces, and life, why do we hear so much about a "good fit" and so little, if anything, about a "good misfit"? Colleges encourage students to seek out the place that matches them; workplaces use algorithms to identify desired employees. Private individuals look for friends and partners with preestablished qualities; social and dating websites use detailed questionnaires and profiles to help them narrow their pool. In their quest for an ideal match, people and institutions disregard the benefits of mismatches.

In 2004, I applied to the New York City Teaching Fellows Program. After participating in an interview event, I received a rejection letter. Determined to become a teacher, I reapplied in 2005. The program accepted reapplications only from applicants whose qualifications had changed—for instance, if they gained relevant experience or earned a degree. I stated in my application that my perseverance was in itself a change in qualifications. I saw no other way to improve my candidacy; I had more than the requisite education and experience.

I received a rejection letter again. Unwilling to give up, I wrote the program director a letter asking why I was turned down; I received a form reply stating that the program does not disclose reasons for rejection. Finally I turned to a retired educator with connections in the school system; upon looking into the matter, he gathered that I had been deemed a mismatch. Perhaps my overall profile—advanced degrees, wide range of interests, varied work history—suggested to the admissions officers that I would not last long in a stressful public school environment. A few conversations later, I was permitted to reapply. This time, everything fell into place, and I entered the program in the summer of 2005. After an intensive summer training, I began teaching at a Brooklyn middle school and taking education courses in the evenings.

My first four years of teaching were filled with accomplishment, challenge, and joy. After this period, I left to write a book; upon completing it, I taught (part-time on paper but more than full-time in reality) for five years at Columbia Secondary School, where I led the philosophy program.[1] After leaving again to write the present book, I accepted a position at a high school in Hungary. I have thus been teaching in public schools for more than nine years, and the teaching continues. Moreover, I found that teaching drew on and invigorated all my interests—including languages, music, literature, philosophy, and education itself. As I developed my teaching chops, I began participating in education discussion on a national and international level—giving talks and interviews, taking part in organizations devoted to literature and the humanities, and learning from people whose knowledge and insight I admired.

Being a "misfit," in other words, prepared me for the job. The incongruities contributed to the work. Not fitting, moreover, I had to find my way; through doing this, I helped students do something similar. Many students find themselves hampered or confused by outside expectations; whether applying for colleges and internships, taking standardized tests, or simply trying to get through a day, they contend with a "system" (or collection of systems) that rewards mental constriction. Some of the most thoughtful and able students struggle with the stated and unstated expectations; perhaps they do not take notes when told to do so, or perhaps their essays depart from the prescribed format and requirements. They must learn to survive while keeping their integrity and verve.

Unlike many anti-establishment critics, I support school with its structures and demands. Yet I have known a climate of blame and fear, which affects everyone from superintendents to prospective students. With inspectors citing schools for bulletin boards that depart from the required formatting, with teachers being rated on the basis of students' test scores (and newspapers publishing the ratings), people throughout the system learn to follow not their own judgment, but what they think will bring the least censure. Like teachers and principals, students receive numerous reminders that "doing well" entails behaving just so—that if given a rubric, they must follow it exactly and literally.

Nonetheless, students find ways into genuine interests and pursuits, which allow them to transcend, exceed, or steer around the requirements. One of my students fell in love with Plato's *Republic*. While others leaned toward Aristotle, he defended Plato with vigor and cheer, explaining how the reasoning led to surprising illuminations. Plato, to him, opened up new ways of looking at justice, government, and the human soul. Another student had a facility for explaining concepts and posing questions; in class discussion, she not only put forth her own views but guided and challenged the conversation. Another student liked to linger after class to discuss philosophical questions. Each of these students approached the subject idiosyncratically; rather than do exactly and only what was expected of them, they looked for meaning. Their "misfitting" became their excellence.

Yet when it came time to apply to college, they, along with others, came under pressure to find a "good fit" (rather than simply a good college). "The most important factor in choosing a college," writes Martha O'Connell, executive director of Colleges That Change Lives, "is *fit*." She advises prospective students to visit college websites, spend a few days on the colleges' campuses, spend time with the students, and try to imagine themselves as part of the community.[2] Peter Van Buskirk, founder and president of Best College Fit, writes that a college is suitable for you if it will: "(1) offer a program of study to match your interests and needs; (2) provide a style of instruction to match the way you like to learn; (3) provide a level of academic rigor to match your aptitude and preparation; (4) offer a community that feels like home to you; and (5) value you for what you do well."[3] All of this advice seems reasonable but also has pitfalls. Should students really look for schools that match their preferences and level exactly, or should they seek some healthy discomfort and challenge? Should they seek places that immediately feel affirming and welcoming, or should they take the risk of strangerhood?

The right answer will vary from person to person—it may be a mixture of answers—but it calls the concept of a "good fit" into question. Students should seek out schools that have programs, departments, and courses that interest them. In that sense, a good fit is essential. Taken to extremes, the concept of a good fit shortchanges both the college and the student; it creates the expectation that if you find the right place, it will feel like home from the start. College is not home, and there is good reason for it not to be. At its best, college provokes new levels of knowledge, thought, understanding, and maturity; this does not happen if students expect comfort. Nor do colleges themselves thrive on excesses of sameness and safety, which turn them into hotels; they need substance, dialogue, and intellectual risk. Bret Stephens writes, "Discomfort is not injury. An intellectual provocation is not a physical assault. It's a stimulus. Over time, it can improve our own arguments, and sometimes even change our minds."[4] Individually and together, we learn from the bare idea, from speech that did not initially seek approval or warm itself in a group.

The trend toward intellectual uniformity on college campuses has worried many educators. Michael S. Roth, president of Wesleyan University, warns that "demonizing people because they have ideas different from your own has always been a temptation, and lately it has become a national contagion. College campuses are not at all immune from it, but this malady is fatal for liberal education." If students expect to be surrounded by like-minded peers, they will not learn how to "respond thoughtfully to points of view different from their own." This state of things, according to Roth, requires concerted response. "We must highlight and enhance the ways that students and faculty members consider alternative perspectives on culture and society," he writes; "we must promote vigorous debate that doesn't degenerate into personal attack."[5] Roth's words apply not only to political debate but to intellectual pursuit overall.

Not only students' own expectations but a "customer service" model has eroded intellectual diversity. In 2015, the Iowa State Senate considered a bill stipulating that professors would be rated solely on the basis of student evaluations—and those with low ratings would be fired.[6] Although this bill did not pass, it represented a troubling tendency. The trend toward treating students as customers—and demanding that professors meet their requests and needs—destroys intellectual challenge. If students can stipulate what they want from a course and professor, and if a professor can be fired for failing to meet these terms, then learning stalls in its tracks. None of us knows in advance exactly what we want to learn and how; it is our teachers who introduce us to the unusual, the unawaited, the uncomfortable; who read passages aloud so that we never forget them; who point out things we would not have seen. They *prevent* the subject matter from fitting us exactly—and, in so doing, reveal its dimensions. A class that fits us perfectly teaches us little.

What awaits students after college, in the working world? With the streamlining and automatization of job applications, many "misfits" will not even be considered for positions that hold promise for them. Many large firms use automated résumé scanners or adhere to standardized procedures. Especially in an employer's market, hiring committees hesitate to take risks, make exceptions, and exercise imagination. In many cases, they already have someone specific in mind; when they do not, they look for someone who will learn the job quickly and fit in without a hitch. According to David D. Perlmutter, dean of the College of Media and Communication at Texas Tech University, academic hiring committees assess not only candidates' qualifications but their cultural fit; applicants have been questioned or tested on such topics as their knowledge of wines, their clothes, their jokes, and their preferred types of recreation. When it comes to the résumé itself, a candidate who appears either inexactly or excessively qualified may be disregarded offhand. [7]

The problem of excessive literalism (as well as excessive interpretation) extends far beyond academic hiring. Employers increasingly use personality tests to screen applicants; while intended to flag those who may be hostile or dangerous to the environment, the tests may also hurt promising individuals. According to Susan J. Stabile, a professor at St. John's University School of Law, personality tests have the potential to screen out good applicants both by favoring conformity and by testing unreliably for honesty. Exceptionally qualified (and thoughtful) applicants may fail the test simply because they did not answer in the expected way. Already in 1956, William H. Whyte warned in *The Organization Man* that personality tests "reward the conformist, the pedestrian, the unimaginative—at the expense of the exceptional individual without whom no society, organization or otherwise, can flourish"; as personality tests gain clout, his words deserve more heed. [8]

Because personality tests are designed to resist gaming, their questions may puzzle those who take them seriously. For example, a practice test offered by the Australia-based Institute of Psychometric Coaching asks the user to respond to a series of statements in one of five ways: "Strongly Agree," "Agree," "Neutral," "Disagree," or "Strongly Disagree." Because of the abstract nature of the statements, they make a definitive answer difficult. For instance, how would I respond to the statement "My goals in life are clear"? I have a clear goal of finishing the current book and finishing the school year; I have vaguer but perhaps stronger goals of persisting with writing and teaching in some form. Beyond that, I am open to surprises. Or what about "If people are rude to me I just shrug it off"? In some cases, I might not notice it; in others, I might shrug it off; and in others, I might brood and worry for a while. [9]

Other tests are even more confusing. The Caliper Profile, created more than fifty years ago and still used today, asks candidates to select, out of four statements, the one that best reflects their viewpoint and the one that least reflects it. A sample question (quoted in a *Forbes* article) reads:

a. Sometimes it's better to lose than to risk hurting someone.
b. I'm generally good at making "small talk."
c. Established practices and/or standards should always be followed.
d. I sometimes lose control of my workday.

What does the first statement mean? What kind of "losing" and "hurting" are at stake here, and what is meant by "sometimes" and "risk"? If the underlying sense is something like, "Sometimes it's better to lose an argument than to risk hurting someone's feelings," then I would wonder: Does "sometimes" indicate an exception? Does the statement suggest that there's a time for arguing something to the end and a time for holding back? (That would be difficult to dispute.) Or does the statement mean that it's *generally* better to place others' feelings above one's own victory in an argument? The ambiguity here might lead some people to disregard (a) entirely and focus on the remaining statements. But their meanings are no clearer. Statement (d) must be true for everyone; no one is always in control of his or her workday. Things come up in the workplace—or outside—that require an unexpected shift of attention. Confused by this statement as well, a candidate might focus on (b) and (c). But what if neither of these seems "most" or "least" true? At this point, all the options will be incorrect, and the chosen response will say little about the person. [10]

In other words, one can be disqualified from a job simply by thinking too carefully about the test questions or answering in a way that does not match what the employers or test makers seek. To make things worse, the tests may not measure much of value. According to University of Iowa scholar Frank Schmidt, who in 1998 conducted (and has subsequently updated) a meta-analysis of a century's worth of productivity data, personality tests rank low in their correlation with subsequent employee productivity. While assessments of general mental ability and integrity correlate strongly with both performance and on-the-job learning, tests of emotional intelligence, agreeableness, "person-organization fit," and "person-job fit" show much weaker correlation.[11] If this is so—if personality tests do not accurately predict future performance—might there not be a larger problem at stake? Might it not be possible that employers, in seeking employees who fit their criteria, ignore the promise inherent in a slight mismatch?

In taking up this question, let us steer clear of absurd extremes. Few wish to hire someone supremely unsuited—whether in qualifications or personality—for a job. Employers assess personality both formally and informally, through tests, interviews, and references. Someone who declares, in an interview, that "libraries are a total waste of resources and space" can reasonably be disqualified from the candidacy for a library staff position. If a particular computer programming position involves daily deadlines, and the applicant says, "I work best on my own schedule," then this person, however qualified otherwise, might not be suited for the work.

In less extreme situations, a mismatch can bring life not only to a workplace but to the worker and the work. "Misfit theory"—now gaining traction in business circles—posits a relation between misfit status and entrepreneurship. According to this argument, people on the fringes of society, such as immigrants, are particularly disposed to seek alternative—and sometimes highly creative—means of employment.[12] But why not bring some of this wisdom into workplaces? Why not regard certain kinds of misfits as assets rather than liabilities? I will now explore several distinct scenarios where a mismatch can enhance the workplace, the worker, and the work. From there I will proceed beyond the workplace.

Let us consider, first of all, the most obvious kinds of mismatch: overqualification and underqualification. Employers commonly assume that an overqualified applicant is not sincerely interested in the job but rather is desperate for work or has a hidden motive for applying. This is not necessarily so. An overqualified applicant may seek a stable job that leaves time and energy for outside projects. This person may be committed to performing the job well—precisely because it allows for other activities. Someone working on a book may welcome a library job (a nonlibrarian position) with light duties and stable hours; such a position is clearly bounded and does not interfere with one's personal life. In addition, the environment might be calm rather than frenzied; at the end of the workday, the employee has ample energy for other things.

What about underqualification? Sometimes a person applies for a job but does not have all the listed skills. In this case, instead of rejecting the applicant offhand, the hiring body can assess whether this person can still do the work. Some people desire responsibilities beyond their immediate qualifications; they find joy in living up to a new challenge. Moreover, some positions require skills that can be gained only through experience in the field; those seeking an initial entry need a chance. It will not do to say, "Because Erica has never done this before, she is unqualified to do it now." The employer should take more into account and consider how to welcome beginners. This would benefit both the employees and the company; the latter would gain new talent as well as reputation. People do not easily forget those who gave them a chance.

When it comes to selecting employees on the basis of personality and temperament, employers should again exercise judgment and imagination. Someone who focuses intensely and meets deadlines may or may not be a good choice for a school principal; much depends on what else the person brings and how tolerant she is of interruptions and aberrations. As for getting along with the "team," much depends on what is meant by "getting along." A workplace need not be monolithic; someone substantially older or younger than the others or someone with a different lifestyle (for instance, who does not go out partying after work) may bring a refreshing perspective. If the applicant shows a willingness to listen to others and participate in the general responsibilities, that is often enough, as far as personality fit goes. The workplace does not have to be a social center.

Some of my most fruitful collaborations have been with people who did not quite fit in: who had projects and responsibilities outside of school, held a different outlook from most, or eschewed group outings and associated with others in their own way. Such people often had strong intellectual grounding; I could learn from them, talk with them about literature and other subjects, and enjoy their presence. In contrast, I have felt at odds with trend-followers, people who believe that the latest is the best. I do not share their thirst for currentness.

But why focus on school and work alone? There is life beyond them—and, with that, extraordinary liberty, within limits. Few can afford to defy all social codes; codes exist to help us understand each other and take part in common events. But when our greatest thought or intuition says, "Break away," and when this does not pose harm, all rests on this departure, as slight as it may be. We participate more strongly when allowed to move this way and that, when allowed to think about what is happening. This allowance is internal, but works of intellect and art enlarge and inform it.

Consider a religious person. Any religion has its standards, norms, and rituals; to some extent, when accepting the religion, a person accepts the norms too. But there is also something sacred about diverging and differing; this keeps the norms from becoming too rigid, literal, bureaucratic, and pat. Judaism, for instance, places great emphasis on family, marriage, child-rearing, and community, but all of this involves solitude. Solitude has a place not only in the culture but in the liturgy and texts; there would be no Judaism without the aloneness of Abraham, Rebecca, Moses, Hannah, Jeremiah, or the Psalms. Some instances of first-person plural in the liturgy originated as first-person singular; for those who know its sources, the singularity remains. Jeremiah 17:14 ("Heal me, O Lord, and I will be healed; save me, and I will be saved; for Thou art my praise") appears in the central Jewish prayer, the Amidah, as "Heal us, O Lord" but retains its individual and personal cry. Over the course of a Shabbat service, there is subtle progression from the "I" to the "We": the early-morning prayers and *piyutim* (liturgical poems) often look inward, focusing on waking up, gratitude for a new day, and gratitude for the soul. José Rolando Matalon, the Senior Rabbi of B'nai Jeshurun in New York City, writes of one of these *piyutim*, "Odeh La-El," that it "provides a window into the great and miraculous journey of the soul to its divine source each night while the worshiper, unaware, sleeps."[13] These layers of solitude, introspection, and mystery fill Jewish liturgy and life.

Religion is by definition transcendent; its tenets, laws, or traditions fail to sum it up. There is always an increase waiting, an understanding that goes beyond our own. The misfit, or seeming misfit, not only helps others to see this, but learns to see beyond herself. I find joy in Torah reading (that is, cantillation), in studying texts, and in leading services; all of this requires extensive solitary preparation. These forms and times of solitude have allowed me to stand my ground and become part of com-

munities; through sticking out slightly, and through following my yearnings, I enter into something larger.

In friendship, too, the misfit not only has a place but brings up treas-
ures. When growing to know each other, two people discover the unusual
in each other, the things that separate each of them from the rest. At some
point, the friendship departs from acquaintanceship or group socializing;
the two people know each other in a particular, unreplicable way. What
others say about them matters less, within the friendship, than what they
know about each other. Each conversation, each occasion spent together
allows for discovery of each other; the misfit can never be fully known or
formulated. In close friendship, all are misfits; they let themselves be
known not for their group approval but for their quirks and gifts, their
pain, humor, and joy. When I think of my strongest and most enduring
friendships, I see how different these friends are from anyone else I
know—yet the difference is in each person, waiting. It comes through in
the friendship itself.

Beyond friendship, the misfit finds glory in private thought. When at
odds with the world (slightly or severely), he has something to think
about; he can analyze the situation at hand, look to literature and art,
ponder a problem, and find a way to strength. Such thoughts require little
money, can be conducted almost everywhere, and need not follow an
external schedule. They can save a situation; if you know how to think
about something from different angles, how to go beyond your immediate
reaction, how to return to things that matter, you can avoid falling into
anger, hurt, and despair. In addition, this kind of thinking opens the
imagination; for some it leads to stories, for others to geometry.

So far in this discussion, I have assumed, or seemed to assume, that
"misfit status" is static—that one is or is not a misfit, especially in a given
situation. This is not so; we have times of fitting in and times of feeling at
odds, even in a single day. We make the mistake of thinking, in the latter
cases, that something has gone wrong, but something may in fact have
gone right. Feeling newly at odds with a situation can be a sign of the
mind maturing, questioning its surroundings, looking for new things. If I
felt, for instance, that I and another person always connected magically,
and then one day I felt that we did not, perhaps it is not necessary anymore to "connect magically" all the time. Perhaps it is enough to come
together with our similarities and differences, to appreciate and hear each
other, to do things together, and even to go separate ways. So, too, with a

workplace: what seems an ideal environment may one day lose some of its charm, and a person may feel out of sorts. This is no disaster: neither a place nor a person can manage to stay charming all the time; moreover, the sense of unsettlement can provoke new ideas and solutions. How do we work with ourselves, with others, and with the situation at hand? The challenge lies in taking this question seriously instead of running away from it.

Outside of work, a person may go through periods of outsiderness: for instance, when mourning, in love, grappling with lost love, or immersed in a project. Why lament this condition? It can allow for necessary retreat. How dreary it would be to fit into a group at all times! There would be nowhere to go, except with the group; nothing to do, except what the group did; and nothing to say, except in preapproved words. The misfit sees the exit but can also come back in; the group, too, depends on these doors for its vitality. By making room for entrances and exits, a society increases its possibilities.

All this said, outsiderness and misfitting need not be ends in themselves. Most of us long for a sense of home; we want to work, live, and think in settings where we do not have to explain and justify ourselves at every turn. These homes can make room for divergence. The misfitting happens on its own, without our bidding. Sometimes our sense of being at odds exposes a larger problem: we may be in the wrong setting, or the setting itself may need changing. But the subtler differences, the times, occasions, or ongoing conditions of standing apart from the group, can bring good after good. There is delight in words and gestures that depart from what we expected and in moods that do not quite match the setting. Life becomes larger; we come to hear not only the known melody but variations, counterpoints, and clashes.

No one fully fits in, and if we could, we would lose our experiences, friends, and questions; our beloved hours of music; our entrance into books. For parts of our day, for survival and dignity, we follow rules, take precautions, and seek shelter; for the rest, in our openings of thought, we can welcome the stranger and the strange (while taking appropriate precautions). These are the hours of inviting a new friend to dinner, listening to a poem, walking along a river, attending a play, figuring out a passage in an unfamiliar language, helping someone in need, speaking with someone on the train, or staying silent on that same train and looking out at the evening fields. Those welcomings rise up into hospitality and wonder. A good life comes—bumpily and unpredictably but faithfully nonetheless—out of years of good misfitting.

# AFTERWORD

This book started as a commentary on words and phrases that, in my view, had been overused and abused. As it took shape, it showed something at stake beyond jargon. Words affect everything from knowledge to dignity. Much of today's discourse cuts up complex phenomena, melts them into platitudes, and molds them into trinkets. To give language a shaking—scrutinizing catchphrases, arresting clichés, proposing alternatives—is to stay intellectually, ethically, and imaginatively alive.

To do this, one must keep some distance from trends. This does not mean retreating into obscurity; a contemporary book deserves to be read, and a new voice to be heard. But a person who thinks independently must, by definition, resist some of the terms of the times; she may go to literature that few are talking about, use words that resist automaticity, and suggest possibilities outside the current fashion.

To work with words is to engage in what the poet Tomas Venclova has called "our lofty science, rife with imperfections."[1] Those I most admire for their work with words are acutely aware of their fallibility and imprecision. Sometimes, to make a point clearly, you have to distort it slightly; the question is how much and in which way, and how to acknowledge your limitations.

I think back on the assignment I gave in my philosophy classes. Two students' pieces (both published in the school's philosophy journal, *Contrariwise*) stand out in my memory and bookshelf; both take up the phrase "well-rounded," which permeates college websites, college application advice, and education discussion overall. Annie Polish, then a junior, subjected the phrase to arch geometrical scrutiny. She pointed out, first of all, that "well-roundedness" may not be desirable, since it "leaves little room for the pointiness of individuality." But even if she aspired toward it, she, a polygon, would never attain it. As the number of a regular polygon's sides approaches infinity, the figure approaches but never becomes a circle. How many sides must she add, then? When can she stop?[2]

Sandra Li, also a junior, lampooned the same phrase through a story about Mr. Square, who goes for a job interview at Shapes Inc. Center in Geometry City. The interviewer, Mr. Oval, rejects him in favor of Ms. Circle, "more of a . . . How do you say it? Well-rounded candidate." Mr. Square learns that he has fallen short; unlike Ms. Circle, who shows "equal excellence in every single conceivable area," he shows "equal inferior excellence in four areas, equal superior excellence in four more areas, and varying degrees of excellence ranging from slightly more than inferior excellence to slightly less than superior excellence for all other skills." As the story grows more absurd, it comes closer to reality. I have heard people speak like Mr. Oval.[3]

Both pieces bring out the relation between individuality and imperfection. The polygon will never be a circle, nor need it try to become one; Mr. Square's "varying degrees of excellence" may prove more interesting than Ms. Circle's "equal excellence in every single conceivable area." Individuality, by its nature, fails to fit rubrics and rating systems; yet this failure is actually the individual's success. Through not fitting in, a person has built-in perspective on societal demands, pressures, fashions, and human nature itself. Difference, if built up and fortified, becomes a home workshop, a place for testing assumptions, finding new expressions, and tinkering with tools and materials.

For all the praise lavished on those who "think outside the box" and "challenge the status quo," our structures, particularly our systems of rating and ranking, reward both popularity and conformity. People judge each other not only by what they have to say, but by their numbers of followers; not only by the substance of their work, but by its status markers. The question then becomes: How do you not only speak clearly but find a forum where you will be heard, without compromising your language or thought? It is all well to speak of "public discussion"—but does such a thing even exist?

It exists, but one must listen for it, just as one must listen for anything. One of the essays of this book is devoted to listening, but there is much more to say about it. First of all, listening is often dismissed as passive or extolled as the key to all awareness. Both extremes are misguided; listening comes in many forms and imperfections. The so-called good listener may actually be a good daydreamer; some of us mix listening with reverie (not always a bad thing).

But even imperfect listening helps a person find a place in the world; the ear and mind take interest in things, remember them, return to them, and bring them into daily life. Poems, speeches, plays, musical compositions, stories read aloud stay with a person and become, in some way, part of his or her character and speech. Through listening, one also notices others: those with a particular voice, rhythm, intonation, sense of humor.

One can also wend one's way into the world by ear, just as Dante and Virgil find their way out of Inferno. Certain places, publications, occasions have an inviting tone; you seek them out, take them in, and eventually participate in them. Journals advise aspiring authors repeatedly, "Please familiarize yourself with our journal before submitting work." This is not a marketing ploy; the person who understands a journal's contents and character will know when and how to enter it—for a journal is not just an assembly of writings, but an orchestration of them.

On a larger scale, listening at its best requires patience and strength. To listen, one must believe that there is something worth hearing to the end, and one must take it in, moment by moment. In listening there can be little skimming; since it happens in time, one must stay with it from start to finish. This requires humility: I cannot decide, in the middle of it, that I have something more important to do. While I am listening, my urges, tasks, and anxieties can wait. I must also put together what I hear— sometimes vigorously and analytically, sometimes gently; sometimes on the spot, sometimes later. Different kinds and stages of listening call for different kinds of thought, but they all ask for something.

Listening requires listening *to* something. It is impossible and undesirable to listen to everything; we must select. Having selected something, we give ourselves over to learning what it holds. Listening counters the culture of reactivity and summary, of branding and name-calling, of banners waving big ideas, of tweets with capital letters and exclamation points. To listen is to admit to incompleteness and imperfection, and thus to sit up taller.

Being listened to is almost as profound as listening; those who sit with us in time, who take in what we say or sing or play (or hold back), remind us that our lives are not exchangeable, our words not dismissible, and that we deserve, here and now, to be marked with someone's attention. This reminder does not go away.

Words and listening have an ancient, inherent relation; it is through close attention that we distinguish groups of sounds and associate them with meaning. In doing so, we affirm that speech has substance, that not a verb is parsed in vain, that humans can stand up to their times through sense and searching.

All the same, listening, however glorious, can be no panacea. First, it comes in so many forms that it has no overarching umbrella; second, it suffers from distractions and interruptions; and third, it does not always come from or lead to good. I would like to end, then, with some thoughts on what it means to live without panacea, even without a modestly big solution, even without a handy little key to life.

To live without panacea is to hear the undertones of words, their shades and contradictions of meaning. The dictionary opens up like an ancient and modern city. In "listening," for instance, one hears both obedience and fame; its two tendencies pull against each other, demanding that we be kings and servants at once. Knowing this pull, understanding listening's contradictions, we can thrill in its imperfections and variations, its own hidden music (since listening has music of its own).

To live without panacea is to read, write, live in liberty—for when speech no longer has to arrive at a grand conclusion, a sweeping summary, a phrase that catches all of humanity in its nets, when allowed to break and build, to test out tones, to weave in and out of light, it shows its mettle. Just as a flute, no longer believed to have miraculous healing powers, can peal forth its melody and timbre; just as the stars, relieved of astrological burden, can offer fascination; so a life without buzzwords, without pat solutions, opens question after question, insight after insight.

The point is not to revel in the thickets of complexity or deny all distilled wisdom. (Living without panacea is no panacea.) Rather, no matter what complexity or simplicity comes along, we can respond to it with full mind. Its complexity, simplicity, popularity, or unpopularity does not force a particular response; we can consider it in its full merit, not expecting it to do anything for us except add to our experience and understanding.

Religion has a place here, too, for those who hold it; to believe in God is not to claim answers or certainties. The Bible and other sacred texts take us into story, poem, question, and awe; one can revel in these texts without taking false certainties from them. Likewise, though differently, an agnostic can live with the unknown, neither closing off all possibility of the divine nor professing false faith. Atheists, too, know a kind of wonder; for many, the empirical world holds endless possibilities.

Literature opens up to the one who lives without panacea; literature tilts, widens, or otherwise alters our view, suggesting that we did not have it quite right. The difference may lie in a sleight of wing. Through literature, one sees the importance of the tilting.

Living without panacea, one can meet others face-to-face, seeing them not only for what they offer us, but also for what they do not; not only for what we perceive in them, but for what we will never know. Dialogue comes alive when it does not have to push a specific conclusion, when it allows for surprises, when it alters, even slightly, the thing we had been planning to say. The good life is not a glib gliding of circles; it has angles, unusual shapes, and confrontation.

Living without panacea, we learn to live with language. Through reading, listening, thinking, and testing out possibilities; speaking with others; entering public discussion; questioning its assumptions and terms; and speaking vigorously against nonsense while also striving for sense, we not only stay alert but rouse the words themselves. Taken seriously, these words will respond in kind.

# NOTES

## INTRODUCTION

1. John Stuart Mill, *On Liberty*, ed. David Bromwich and George Kateb (New Haven: Yale University Press, 2003), 102.

2. George Orwell, "Politics and the English Language," in *A Collection of Essays* (New York: Harcourt, 1981), 156.

3. "All language is a play on words" is a quotation from my piece "November Love Letter," *Yale Literary Magazine* (Fall 1991): 26–27.

4. The Republic of Užupis, *Constitution of the Republic of Užupis*, Užupis Everywhere website, http://uzhupisembassy.eu/uzhupis-constitution/.

## I. TAKE AWAY THE TAKEAWAY

1. The present anecdote is loosely based on a true story that one of my students told in political philosophy class. We were discussing Hannah Arendt's statement (in *The Human Condition*) that "greatness has given way to charm everywhere"; the student described a recent interview to illustrate Arendt's point. See Arendt, *The Human Condition*, 2nd ed. (Chicago: University of Chicago Press, 1998), 52.

2. Herman Melville, *Moby-Dick* (New York: Norton, 2002), 116.

3. *OED Online*, s.v. "takeaway (*n.*)," definition 6 (Oxford University Press, January 2018), accessed February 28, 2018, http://www.oed.com/view/Entry/197161?rskey=W4LYNW&result=2.

4. Mike Twohy, cartoon, *New Yorker*, November 26, 2012.

5. Dallas Independent School District, *Teacher Performance Rubric: Overview of Domains and Indicators* (Dallas: Dallas ISD, 2014), 6.

6. David Orr, *The Road Not Taken: Finding America in the Poem Everyone Loves and Almost Everyone Gets Wrong* (New York: Penguin, 2015), 71–72.

7. Jay Parini, *Robert Frost: A Life* (New York: Henry Holt, 1999), 153–55; Orr, *The Road Not Taken*, 76–82.

8. Student Achievement Partners, "The Road Not Taken" (lesson plan), *Achieve the Core*, September 29, 2014, revised February 23, 2016, https:// achievethecore.org/page/2641/the-road-not-taken.

9. Ken Robinson, "Do Schools Kill Creativity?" *TED*, February 2006, https:/ /www.ted.com/talks/ken_robinson_says_schools_kill_creativity#t-1135025.

10. Ken Robinson, *Out of Our Minds: The Power of Being Creative*, 3rd ed. (Chichester, UK: Capstone, 2017), 52–53.

11. Ibid., 85–88.

12. William Deresiewicz, *Excellent Sheep: The Miseducation of the American Elite and the Way to a Meaningful Life* (New York: Free Press, 2014).

13. Amy Cuddy, "Your Body Language May Shape Who You Are" (originally titled "Your Body Language Shapes Who You Are"), *TEDGlobal 2012*, filmed June 2012, https://www.ted.com/talks/amy_cuddy_your_body_language_ shapes_who_you_are.

14. Cuddy, "Your Body Language May Shape Who You Are"; Dana R. Carney, Amy J. C. Cuddy, and Andy J. Yap, "Power Posing: Brief Nonverbal Displays Affect Neuroendocrine Levels and Risk Tolerance," *Psychological Science* 21, no. 10 (2010): 1363–68; Joe Simmons and Uri Simonsohn, "Power Posing: Reassessing the Evidence Behind the Most Powerful TED Talk," *Data Colada* (blog), May 8, 2015, http://datacolada.org/37; Eva Ranehill et al., "Assessing the Robustness of Power Posing: No Effect on Hormones and Risk Tolerance in a Large Sample of Men and Women," *Psychological Science* 26, no. 5 (May 2015): 653–56; Katie E. Garrison, David Tang, and Brandon J. Schmeichel, "Embodying Power: A Preregistered Replication and Extension of the Power Pose Effect," *Social Psychological and Personality Science* 7, no. 7 (September 2016): 623–30; Jesse Singal, "'Power Posing' Co-Author: 'I Do Not Believe That "Power Pose" Effects Are Real,'" The Cut, *New York Magazine*, September 26, 2016; Joseph Cesario, Kai J. Jonas, and Carney, "CRSP Special Issue on Power Poses: What Was the Point and What Did We Learn?" *Comprehensive Results in Social Psychology* 2, no. 1 (2017): 1–5; Susan Dominus, "When the Revolution Came for Amy Cuddy," *New York Times*, October 18, 2017.

15. [TED], "TEDx Speaker Guide," accessed February 14, 2018, https:// storage.ted.com/tedx/manuals/tedx_speaker_guide.pdf.

16. Cuddy, "Your Body Language May Shape Who You Are."

17. Andrew Gelman, "Low Power Pose Update: TED Goes All-In," *Statistical Modeling, Causal Inference, and Social Science* (blog), February 28, 2017, http://andrewgelman.com/2017/02/28/low-power-pose-update-ted-goes/.

18. Nathan Heller, "Listen and Learn," *New Yorker*, July 9, 2012; Alex Pareene, "Don't Mention Income Inequality Please, We're Entrepreneurs," *Salon*, May 21, 2012; Jason Kehe, "Wired's Guide to Crafting the Perfect TED Talk," *Wired*, April 16, 2013.

19. Andrew Gelman and Kaiser Fung, "The Power of the 'Power Pose,'" *Slate*, January 19, 2016.

20. "Dr. No Money: The Broken Science Funding System" (editorial), *Scientific American*, May 11, 2011.

21. John Oliver, "Peeple" (segment), *Last Week Tonight*, episode 53, October 4, 2015; Jessica Condit, "Peeple Is Boring," Engadget.com, March 9, 2016, https://www.engadget.com/2016/03/09/peeple-is-boring/.

22. Daniel Sanchez, "Why Ratings and Reviews Are for Products, Not People," *The Sociable*, October 17, 2017, https://sociable.co/social-media/ratings-reviews-products/ .

## 2. CHANGE, OUR FALSE GOD

1. Andrew Sturdy and Christopher Grey, "Beneath and Beyond Organizational Change Management: Exploring Alternatives," *Organization* 10, no. 4 (2003): 651–62.

2. For more on e-books' simulations of page-turning, see Chaoran Fan, Haisheng Li, and Yannan Bai, "Realistic Page-Turning of Electronic Books," *Proceedings of SPIE* 9069, Fifth International Conference on Graphic and Image Processing (ICGIP 2013), 906920 (January 10, 2014); doi: 10.1117/12.2050888, https://doi.org/10.1117/12.2050888.

3. One Laptop per Child, "Mission," One Laptop per Child website, http://one.laptop.org/about/mission.

4. Homer, *Iliad*, trans. Richmond Lattimore (Chicago: University of Chicago Press, 2011), 75; Homer, *Iliad*, trans. Robert Fagles (New York: Penguin, 1998), 77.

5. Elisa Villanueva Beard, "Fighting the Wrong Enemy" (speech), TFA Alumni Gathering, July 18, 2013, http://www.teachforamerica.org/blog/fighting-wrong-enemy; Beard, "How I Define the Status Quo," Teach For America website, July 31, 2013, http://www.teachforamerica.org/top-stories/elisa-villanueva-beard-how-i-define-status-quo.

6. *Online Etymology Dictionary*, s.v. "change (*v.*)," accessed February 28, 2018, https://www.etymonline.com/word/change; *OED Online*, s.v. "change

(*n.*)," accessed February 28, 2018, http://www.oed.com/view/Entry/30467? rskey=FepAqi&result=1.

7. *Online Etymology Dictionary*, s.v. "mutation (*n.*)," accessed February 28, 2018, https://www.etymonline.com/word/mutation; s.v. "*-mei" (proto-Indo-European root), accessed February 28, 2018, https://www.etymonline.com/word/ *mei-; *OED Online*, s.v. "mutation (*n.*)" accessed February 28, 2018, http:// www.oed.com/view/Entry/124296?redirectedFrom=mutation.

8. Flannery O'Connor, *Wise Blood* (New York: Noonday, 1967), [5].


# 3. THE UBIQUITOUS TEAM


1. Margaret Buchman, "Beyond the Lonely, Choosing Will: Professional Development in Teacher Thinking," *Teachers College Record* 91, no. 4 (1990): 508.

2. Mieke Clement and Katrine Staessens, "The Professional Development of Primary School Teachers and the Tension between Autonomy and Collegiality," in *School Culture, School Improvement, and Teacher Development*, ed. F. Kieviet and R. Vandenberghe (Leiden: DSWO Press, 1993), 129–52. For one of many instances of the phrase "Good teachers are team players," see Jerry Boyle, *It's All About People Skills: Surviving Challenges in the Classroom* (Lanham, MD: Rowman & Littlefield Education, 2011), 11.

3. *Online Etymology Dictionary*, s.v. "team (*n.*)," accessed February 11, 2018, http://etymonline.com/index.php?allowed_in_frame=0&search=team.

4. *OED Online*, s.v. "team (*n.*)," definitions 1a, 1b, 3a, 4b, and 5a, accessed February 11, 2018, http://www.oed.com/view/Entry/198373?rskey=ChH3QU& result=1.

5. William Shakespeare, *A Midsummer Night's Dream*, V.i.374; *All's Well That Ends Well*, I.iii.44; *Henry IV Part I*, III.i.214; *Romeo and Juliet*, I.iv.57; *The Two Gentlemen of Verona*, III.i.264; *Venus and Adonis*, 179; John Fletcher and William Shakespeare, *The Two Noble Kinsmen*, I.ii.59. References are to act, scene, and line; the line numbers correspond with those in the New Penguin Shakespeare Series, ed. Terence Spencer (New York: Penguin, 1937–1959).

6. Andrew Gelman, "Division of Labor and a Pizzagate Solution," *Statistical Modeling, Causal Inference, and Social Science* (blog), February 23, 2017, http:/ /andrewgelman.com/2017/02/23/division-labor-pizzagate-solution/.

7. Amy Edmonson, *Teaming: How Organizations Learn, Innovate, and Compete in the Knowledge Economy* (New York: Wiley, 2012), 12.

8. Mike Isaac, "Inside Uber's Aggressive, Unrestrained Workplace Culture," *New York Times*, February 22, 2017.

9. David R. Seibold, Paul Kang, Bernadette M. Gailliard, and Jody Jahn, "Communication That Damages Teamwork: The Dark Side of Teams," in *Destructive Organizational Communication: Processes, Consequences, and Constructive Ways of Organizing*, ed. Pamela Lutgen-Sandvik and Beverly Davenport Sypher (New York: Routledge, 2009), 267–90; Jane O'Reilly, Sandra L. Robinson, Jennifer L. Berdahl, and Sara Banki, "Is Negative Attention Better Than No Attention? The Comparative Effects of Ostracism and Harassment at Work," *Organization Science* 26, no. 3 (2015): 774–93.

10. J. Richard Hackman, "Why Teams Don't Work," interview with Diane Coutu, *Harvard Business Review*, May 2009.

11. Joseph P. Lash, *Helen and Teacher: The Story of Helen Keller and Anne Sullivan Macy* (New York: Delacorte, 1980), 489.

## 4. IS LISTENING PASSIVE?

1. John Cunningham, "Remembering Alexander Slobodyanik on First Night," NJ.com, December 19, 2008, http://www.nj.com/morristown/firstnight/index.ssf/2008/12/a_first_night_to_remember_alex.html; Cunningham, *The Miracle on South Street: The Story of Morristown's Community Theatre* (Morristown, NJ: South Street Theatre Co., 2000); Mayo Performing Arts Center, "Twenty Memorable Events in MPAC History," MPAC website, http://www.mayoarts.org/about/20-memorable-events-in-mpac-history.

2. Plutarch, "On Listening to Lectures," in *Moralia*, vol. 1, trans. F. C. Babbitt (Cambridge, MA: Harvard University Press, 1927), 243–45.

3. Ibid., 227.

4. Craig Lambert, "Twilight of the Lecture," *Harvard Magazine*, March–April 2012.

5. *OED Online*, s.v. "listen (*v.*)," definition 2a, accessed February 28, 2018, http://www.oed.com/view/Entry/109008?rskey=HOjFAC&result=2.

6. Roland Barthes and Richard Havas, "Listening," in Barthes, *The Responsibility of Forms: Critical Essays on Music, Art, and Representation*, trans. Richard Howard (New York: Hill and Wang, 1984), 245–46, 252.

7. Joshua Jacobson, *Chanting the Hebrew Bible: The Complete Guide to the Art of Cantillation* (Philadelphia: Jewish Publication Society, 2002); Cantor Perry Fine, Advanced Cantillation (yearlong course, 2016–2017), H. L. Miller Cantorial School, Jewish Theological Seminary.

8. *Theological Dictionary of the Old Testament*, vol. 15 (Grand Rapids, MI: Eerdmans, 2006), s.v. "šāma'," 273–74.

9. Although people commonly say, for instance, "Jacob is having his bar mitzvah," it is more accurate to say, "Jacob is becoming a bar mitzvah." The bar

or bat mitzvah is the young person who has attained the age of obligation (thirteen for boys, twelve for girls) under Jewish law.

10. Lewis Glinert, "Putting Back the Meaning into Leyning," *L'eylah* 32 (September 1991): 16–18.

11. Numbers 35:5 (Jewish Publication Society of America Tanakh, 1985).

12. There is no single "correct" melody for the *te'amim*; they vary from person to person, synagogue to synagogue, tradition to tradition, and place to place. Nor can musical notation precisely render the rhythm and intonation. The melody that appears here is an approximation of the way I would chant the verse.

13. For more on stepping segments, see Jacobson, *Chanting the Hebrew Bible*, 72–75.

14. "Numbers 35:5" (mp3 recording), chanted by Diana Senechal, Diana Senechal website, http://www.dianasenechal.com/numbers35_5.mp3.

15. Danny Shilan, "Renewing the Spirit," *Kol Torah* 19, no. 33 (Summer 2010).

16. Dante Alighieri, *Purgatorio* 18:143–45, *The Divine Comedy*, trans. Allen Mandelbaum (New York: Everyman's Library, 1995), 302.

17. See, for example, the description of the "Distinguished" level in item 3b of the Danielson Framework, "Using Questioning and Discussion Techniques": "The teacher uses a variety or series of questions or prompts to challenge students cognitively, advance high-level thinking and discourse, and promote metacognition. Students formulate many questions, initiate topics, challenge one another's thinking, and make unsolicited contributions. Students themselves ensure that all voices are heard in the discussion." Charlotte Danielson, *The Framework for Teaching: Evaluation Instrument*, 2013 edition, https://www.danielsongroup.org/framework/.

18. See, for instance, Loraine Corrie, *Investigating Troublesome Classroom Behavior: Practical Tools for Teachers* (New York: RoutledgeFarmer, 2001), 143; Sue Cowley, *How to Survive Your First Year in Teaching* (London: Bloomsbury Education, 2013), 56; Sue Roffey, *The New Teacher's Survival Guide to Behaviour*, 2nd ed. (London: Sage, 2011), 58.

19. Plutarch, "On Listening to Lectures," 209.

## 5. RESEARCH HAS SHOWN—JUST WHAT, EXACTLY?

1. Virginia P. Collier and Wayne P. Thomas, "How Quickly Can Immigrants Become Proficient in School English?" *Journal of Educational Issues of Language Minority Students* 5 (Fall 1989): 26–38, esp. 28; see also Kenji Hakuta, Yuko Goto Butler, and Daria Witt, "How Long Does It Take English Learners to

Attain Proficiency?" [Santa Barbara]: University of California Linguistic Minority Research Institute, 2000.

2. H. J. Eysenck and Sybil B. G. Eysenck, "On the Unitary Nature of Extraversion," *Acta Psychologica* 26 (1967): 383–90.

3. Brian Little, *Me, Myself, and Us: The Science of Personality and the Art of Well-Being* (New York: Public Affairs, 2014), 49.

4. Susan Cain, *Quiet: The Power of Introverts in a World That Can't Stop Talking* (New York: Crown, 2012), 124.

5. Eysenck and Eysenck, "On the Unitary Nature," 384.

6. Ibid., 388.

7. Ibid.

8. British Broadcasting Service, "Lemon Juice Experiment," *Science: Human Body and Mind*, http://www.bbc.co.uk/science/humanbody/mind/articles/personalityandindividuality/lemons.shtml; Melissa Dahl, "Here's a Test for Introversion You Can Do When You're Home, Being Introverted," The Cut, *New York Magazine*, April 21, 2016.

9. K. Anders Ericsson, Ralf Th. Krampe, and Clemens Tesch-Römer, "The Role of Deliberate Practice in the Acquisition of Expert Performance," *Psychological Review* 100, no. 3 (1993): 363–406; see 368, 370, 393–94.

10. Ibid., 373–74.

11. Ibid., 374–80.

12. Ibid., 381–87.

13. Ibid., 393.

14. Malcolm Gladwell, *Outliers: The Story of Success* (New York: Little, Brown, 2008), 41–42, 56.

15. Paul Tough, *How Children Succeed: Grit, Curiosity, and the Hidden Power of Character* (New York: Houghton Mifflin Harcourt, 2012); Angela Duckworth, "Grit: The Power of Passion and Perseverance" (speech), *TED Talks Education*, April 2013; MacArthur Fellows Program, "Angela Duckworth," MacArthur Foundation website, September 25, 2013, https://www.macfound.org/fellows/889/.

16. Angela Duckworth, *Grit: The Power of Passion and Perseverance* (New York: Scribner, 2016), 8; [Duckworth], "12-Item Grit Scale," http://www.sas.upenn.edu/~duckwort/images/12-item%20Grit%20Scale.05312011.pdf; Duckworth and David Scott Yeager, "Measurement Matters: Assessing Personal Qualities Other Than Cognitive Ability for Educational Purposes," *Educational Researcher* 44, no. 4 (May 2015): 237–51; Daniel T. Willingham, "'Grit' Is Trendy, but Can It Be Taught?" *American Educator*, Summer 2016, 28–32, 44; Kristin Ozelli, "Should Grit Be Taught and Tested in School?" *Scientific American*, July 1, 2016.

17.  Kate Zernike, "Testing for Joy and Grit?: Schools Nationwide Push to Measure Students' Emotional Skills," *New York Times*, February 29, 2016.

18.  Jesse Singal, "Psychology's Favorite Tool for Measuring Racism Isn't Up to the Job," The Cut, *New York Magazine*, January 11, 2017; Gladwell, *Blink: The Power of Thinking Without Thinking* (New York: Little, Brown, 2005), 85.

19.  Singal, "Psychology's Favorite Tool."

20.  German Lopez, "For Years, This Popular Test Measured Anyone's Racial Bias. But It Might Not Work After All," *Vox*, March 7, 2017; Olivia Goldhill, "The World Is Relying on a Flawed Psychological Test to Fight Racism," *Quartz*, December 3, 2017; Singal, "The Creators of the Implicit Association Test Should Get Their Story Straight," Daily Intelligencer, *New York Magazine*, December 5, 2017.

21.  Project Implicit, "Education," https://implicit.harvard.edu/implicit/education.html; "Ethical Considerations," https://implicit.harvard.edu/implicit/ethics.html.

## 6. SOCIAL AND UNSOCIAL JUSTICE

1.  Vladimir Mayakovsky, *Oblako v shtanakh: Tetraptikh*, 2nd ed., uncensored ([Moscow]: ASIS, [1918]); my translation.

2.  Andy McSmith, *Fear and the Muse Kept Watch: The Russian Masters— from Akhmatova and Pasternak to Shostakovich and Eisenstein—Under Stalin* (New York: New Press, 2015), 32–53.

3.  David Burliuk, Alexander Kruchenykh, Vladimir Mayakovsky, and Viktor Khlebnikov, "Poshchechina obshchestvennomu vkusu" ("A Slap in the Face of Public Taste"), first issued 1912; my translation. Khlebnikov did not contribute to the writing of the manifesto, although he appears as one of the signatories. The full Russian text is available at Wikimedia Commons.

4.  Edward James Brown, *Mayakovsky: A Poet in the Revolution* (Princeton, NJ: Princeton University Press, 1973), 181.

5.  Vladimir Mayakovsky, "Khoroshee otnoshenie k loshadiam," *Novaia zhizn'*, July 9, 1918; my translation.

6.  *Online Etymology Dictionary*, s.v. "justice (*n.*)," accessed February 28, 2016, https://www.etymonline.com/word/justice.

7.  John Rawls, *A Theory of Justice* (Cambridge, MA: Belknap, 2005), 20.

8.  Plato, *Republic* 434c.

9.  Plato, *Republic* 443d; quotation from Plato, *Republic*, trans. G. M. A. Grube, rev. C. D. C. Reeve, 2nd ed. (Indianapolis: Hackett, 1992), 119.

10.  David Bromwich, "Moral Imagination," in *Moral Imagination: Essays* (Princeton, NJ: Princeton University Press, 2014), 39.

11. Aristotle, *Nicomachean Ethics* 8.3, 8.13, 9.3.

12. Martin Buber, *I and Thou*, trans. Ronald Gregor Smith (New York: Scribner, 2000), 31, 43.

13. Martin Luther King Jr., "Letter from a Birmingham Jail," The Martin Luther King, Jr. Research and Education Institute, Stanford University, https://kinginstitute.stanford.edu/king-papers/documents/letter-birmingham-jail.

14. Katharine Q. Seelye, "Protesters Disrupt Speech by 'Bell Curve' Author at Vermont College," *New York Times*, March 3, 2017.

15. Allison Stanger, "Understanding the Angry Mob at Middlebury That Gave Me a Concussion," *New York Times*, March 13, 2017; Will DiGravio et al., "Discord at Middlebury: Students on the Anti-Murray Protests," *New York Times*, March 7, 2017.

16. John Rawls, *Political Liberalism*, expanded ed. (New York: Columbia University Press, 2005), 212–54.

17. Stanger, "Understanding the Angry Mob."

18. Pew Research Center, "Political Polarization in the American Public," June 12, 2014, http://www.people-press.org/2014/06/12/political-polarization-in-the-american-public/.

## 7. THE TOXICITY OF "TOXIC"

1. Lillian Glass, *Toxic People: Ten Ways of Dealing with People Who Make Your Life Miserable* (New York: Simon and Schuster, 1995); David Gillespie, *Taming Toxic People: The Science of Identifying and Dealing with Psychopaths at Work and at Home* (Sydney: Macmillan Australia, 2017); Susan Forward and Craig Buck, *Toxic Parents: Overcoming Their Hurtful Legacy and Reclaiming Your Life* (New York: Bantam, 2002); Liz Ryan, "How to Get Toxic People Out of Your Life," *Forbes*, June 15, 2017; Marcel Schwantes, "Six Toxic Types of People You Need to Cut from Your Life Right Now," *Inc.*, February 9, 2017.

2. Glass, *Toxic People*, 12.

3. Ibid., 72–77, 86, 93–95, 115.

4. Zoe Weiner, "Seven Tips for Eliminating Toxic People from Your Life," *Mental Floss*, March 22, 2017, http://mentalfloss.com/article/93521/7-tips-eliminating-toxic-people-your-life.

5. Schwantes, "Six Toxic Types of People."

6. The back cover of *Toxic People* states that Glass "coined the phrase 'toxic people' used in today's vernacular," yet psychologist Jerry Greenwald wrote of "toxic" and "nourishing" people in his 1974 book *Be the Person You Were Meant to Be: Antidotes to Living* (New York: Simon and Schuster, 1974).

7. *Online Etymology Dictionary*, s.v. "toxic (*adj.*)," accessed February 18, 2018, http://www.etymonline.com/word/toxic.

8. Donald Trump, Twitter feed, August 17, 2017, accessed February 18, 2018, https://twitter.com/realdonaldtrump/status/898136462385979392?lang=en.

9. Rex Huppke, "Trump, the Toxic President. When Will Republicans Have the Sense to Run?" *Chicago Tribune*, August 18, 2017.

10. David Brooks, "The Siege Mentality Problem," *New York Times*, November 13, 2017.

11. George Saunders, "Winky," in *Pastoralia: Stories* (New York: Riverhead, 2000), 69–88.

12. László Krasznahorkai, *Herman: "The Game Warden" and "The Death of a Craft,"* trans. John Batki, in *The Last Wolf; and Herman: "The Game Warden," "The Death of a Craft"* (New York: New Directions, 2016), 7–52.

## 8. THE SPRINGS OF CREATIVITY

1. Robin Fogarty, "Creativity: The Premier Skill of the 21st Century," *P21 Blog*, http://www.p21.org/news-events/p21blog/1118; Organization for Economic Co-operation and Development, Centre for Educational Research and Innovation, *Innovating to Learn, Learning to Innovate* (Paris: OECD, 2008), 48, 197, 225–228; Kyung Hee Kim, "The Creativity Crisis: The Decrease in Creative Thinking Scores on the Torrance Tests of Creative Thinking," *Creativity Research Journal* 23, no. 4 (2011): 285–95; Po Bronson and Ashley Merryman, "The Creativity Crisis," *Newsweek*, July 10, 2010.

2. Council on Competitiveness, *Innovate America: Thriving in a World of Challenge and Change*, report of the 2004 National Innovation Initiative Summit, Washington, D.C. (published May 2005), http://www.compete.org/reports/all/202.

3. Barry Staw, "Why No One Really Wants Creativity," in *Creative Action in Organizations: Ivory Tower Visions and Real World Voices*, ed. Cameron Ford and Dennis Gioia (Thousand Oaks, CA: Sage, 1995), 161–66, quotes from 164–65; see also Jessica Olien, "Inside the Box: People Don't Actually Like Creativity," *Slate*, December 6, 2013, http://www.slate.com/articles/health_and_science/science/2013/12/creativity_is_rejected_teachers_and_bosses_don_t_value_out_of_the_box_thinking.html.

4. Scholastic Testing Service, "Torrance Tests of Creative Thinking (TTCT)," accessed February 18, 2018, http://www.ststesting.com/ngifted.html. For Torrance's cautions regarding the use of the tests, and for John Baer's critique of their overuse, see Baer, "How Divergent Thinking Tests Mislead Us:

Are the Torrance Tests Still Relevant in the 21st Century? The Division 10 Debate," *Psychology of Aesthetics, Creativity, and the Arts* 5, no. 4 (2011): 309–13.

5. Alfred North Whitehead, *Process and Reality* (New York: Free Press, 1978), 20, 164.

6. Liane Gabora, "Honing Theory: A Complex Systems Framework for Creativity," *Nonlinear Dynamics, Psychology, and Life Sciences* 21, no. 1 (January 2017): 35–88.

7. Ken Robinson, *Out of Our Minds: The Power of Being Creative*, 3rd ed. (Chichester, UK: Capstone, 2017), 3.

8. Doreen Virtue, *The Courage to Be Creative: How to Believe in Yourself, Your Dreams and Ideas, and Your Creative Career Path* (Carlsbad, CA: Hay House, 2016), 3.

9. Tom Kelley and David Kelley, *Creative Confidence: Unleashing the Creative Potential within Us All* (New York: Crown Business, 2013), 2.

10. G. K. Chesterton, "The Fallacy of Success," in *All Things Considered* (New York: J. Lane, 1913), 23–24.

11. Diann Daniel, "Microsoft's Culture of Innovation: An Interview with Tony Scott," *CIO*, November 14, 2008.

12. Timothy B. Lee, "How Amazon Innovates in Ways That Apple and Google Can't," *Vox*, December 28, 2016, https://www.vox.com/new-money/2016/12/28/13889840/amazon-innovation-google-apple.

13. Henry Petroski, *Invention by Design: How Engineers Get from Thought to Thing* (Cambridge, MA: Harvard University Press, 1996), 11.

14. Charles Fischer, telephone stand, U.S. Patent 1,371,747, filed May 20, 1919, and issued March 15, 1921 (The United States Patent and Trademark Office), http://www.uspto.gov.

15. Charles Fischer, take-up spring, U.S. Patent 1,578,817, filed September 17, 1924, and issued March 30, 1926 (The United States Patent and Trademark Office), http://www.uspto.gov.

16. Robert Charles Fischer, comment on Diana Senechal, "The Cardinal Book Prop," *Take Away the Takeaway* (blog), March 6, 2017, https://dianasenechal.wordpress.com/2017/02/25/the-cardinal-book-prop/#comment-5956.

17. Miranda Wilson, *Cello Practice, Cello Performance* (Lanham, MD: Rowman & Littlefield, 2015), 27.

## 9. IN PRAISE OF MIXED MINDSETS

1. For more on incremental theory (which Dweck later reframed as "growth mindset"), see Carol S. Dweck, *Self-Theories: Their Role in Motivation, Personality, and Development* (New York: Psychology Press, 2000).

2. Mindset Works, "Assess Your Mindset to Begin Your Journey Today," Mindset Works website, http://blog.mindsetworks.com/what-s-my-mindset.

3. Claudia M. Mueller and Dweck, "Praise for Intelligence Can Undermine Children's Motivation and Performance," *Journal of Personality and Social Psychology* 75, no. 1 (1998): 33–52; Dweck, *Mindset: The New Psychology of Success* (New York: Random House, 2006); Janet Rae-Dupree, "If You're Open to Growth, You Tend to Grow," *New York Times*, July 6, 2008; Dweck, "Mindsets: Developing Talent through a Growth Mindset," *Olympic Coach* 21, no. 1 (Winter 2009): 4–7; David Paunescu, Gregory M. Walton, Dweck et al., "Mind-Set Interventions Are a Scalable Treatment for Academic Underachievement," *Psychological Science* 26, no. 6 (June 2015): 784–93.

4. Mueller and Dweck, "Praise for Intelligence," 48.

5. Education Week Research Center, *Mindset in the Classroom: A National Study of K–12 Teachers* (Bethesda, MD: Editorial Projects in Education, 2016); James Hamblin, "100 Percent Is Overrated," *Atlantic*, June 30, 2016. For a video of a growth mindset cheer performed by third graders, see Cardinal Leger, "Growth Mindset Cheer!" (video), YouTube, April 20, 2015, https://www.youtube.com/watch?v=UgCdWuGZyMU.

6. Anya Kamenetz, "How to Apply the Brain Science of Resilience to the Classroom," *NPREd*, June 12, 2017; Michael P. Kilgard, Amanda Reed et al., "Cortical Map Plasticity Improves Learning but Is Not Necessary for Improved Performance," *Neuron* 70, no. 1 (April 14, 2011): 121–31.

7. Dweck, "Growth Mindset Is on a Firm Foundation, but We're Still Building the House," *Mindset Scholars Network Blog*, January 18, 2017, http://mindsetscholarsnetwork.org/growth-mindset-firm-foundation-still-building-house/; Jesse Singal, "Is Mindset Theory Really in Trouble?" The Cut, *New York Magazine*, January 18, 2017; Dweck, "Carol Dweck Revisits the 'Growth Mindset,'" *Education Week*, September 22, 2015; David S. Yeager, Dave Paunesku, Gregory M. Walton, and Dweck, "How Can We Instill Productive Mindsets at Scale? A Review of the Evidence and an Initial R&D Agenda," white paper prepared for the White House meeting on "Excellence in Education: The Importance of Academic Mindsets," rev. June 10, 2013, https://labs.la.utexas.edu/adrg/files/2013/12/Yeager-et-al-RD-agenda-6-10-131.pdf, 18.

8. Dweck, "Carol Dweck Revisits the 'Growth Mindset.'"

9. Dweck, *Mindset: The New Psychology of Success*, updated ed. (New York: Ballantine, 2016), 151.

10. See, for instance, Richard E. Nisbett, *Intelligence and How to Get It: Why Schools and Cultures Count* (New York: Norton, 2009); *Handbook of Intelligence: Evolutionary Theory, Historical Perspective, and Current Concepts*, ed. Sam Goldstein, Dana Princiotta, and Jack A. Nagieri (New York: Springer, 2015).

## 10. WHAT DO WE MEAN BY "WE"?

1. See, for instance, UC Davis Student Health and Counseling Services, "Why Pronouns Are Important," UC Davis website, March 17, 2017, https://shcs.ucdavis.edu/blog/archive/why-pronouns-are-important; Meg P. Bernhard, "Students Indicate Preferred Gender Pronouns at Registration," *Harvard Crimson*, September 2, 2015.

2. David Bromwich, *Politics by Other Means: Higher Education and Group Thinking* (New Haven, CT: Yale University Press, 1992), 72.

3. Ibid., 194–95.

4. Donald Trump, Ohio rally speech, July 25, 2017, *Time*, http://time.com/4874161/donald-trump-transcript-youngstown-ohio/.

5. E. M. White, "Hillary Clinton Speaks at the Ohio Democratic Party Legacy Dinner," March 13, 2016, https://hillaryspeeches.com/2016/03/13/watch-live-hillary-clinton-speech-at-the-ohio-democratic-party-legacy-dinner/.

6. Susan Cain, "Must Great Leaders Be Gregarious?" *New York Times*, September 15, 2012; Helene Cooper and Abby Goodnough, "Over Beers, No Apologies, but Plans to Have Lunch," *New York Times*, July 30, 2009; Nancy Ancowitz, "Bill Clinton's Innie: Insights for Introverts During Inauguration Week," *Psychology Today*, January 28, 2013; Ancowitz, "Is Obama an Introvert? Introvert or Extrovert? Maybe Only Bo Knows for Sure," *Psychology Today*, October 15, 2010.

7. Susan T. Fiske, "A Call to Change Science's Culture of Shaming," *Observer* (Association for Psychological Science), October 31, 2016; Jesse Singal, "Inside Psychology's 'Methodological Terrorism' Debate," The Cut, *New York Magazine*, October 12, 2016.

8. "Plucky," comment on Andrew Gelman, "What Has Happened Down Here Is the Winds Have Changed," *Statistical Modeling, Causal Inference, and Social Science* (blog), September 21, 2016, http://andrewgelman.com/2016/09/21/what-has-happened-down-here-is-the-winds-have-changed/#comment-314819.

9. David Brooks, "The Glory of Democracy," *New York Times*, December 17, 2017.

10. Dennis Patrick Slattery, "And Who to Know? Monuments, Text and the Trope of Time in William Faulkner's *Absalom, Absalom!*" in *A Limbo of Shards: Essays on Memory Myth and Metaphor* (Lincoln, NE: iUniverse, 2007), 11; Gaston Bachelard, *On Poetic Imagination and Reverie*, trans. Colette Gaudin (Dallas: Spring Publications, 1987), 15.

11. Robert Frost, "The Oven Bird," in *The Poetry of Robert Frost: The Collected Poems, Complete and Unabridged*, ed. Edward Connery Lathem (New York: Henry Holt, 1979), 119–20; John Hollander, lecture delivered at master class for benefactors of the Academy of American Poets, February 9, 1997, https://www.poets.org/poetsorg/text/close-look-robert-frost.

12. Martin Buber, *I and Thou*, trans. Ronald Gregor Smith (New York: Scribner's, 1958), 43.

## 11. A GOOD MISFIT

1. For more on these five years at Columbia Secondary School, see my article "You Are Embarked: How a Philosophy Curriculum Took Shape and Took Off," *American Educator*, Spring 2015, 18–23.

2. Martha O'Connell, "How to Choose a College That's Right for You," NPR Special Series: The College Admissions Game, February 21, 2007, https://www.npr.org/2010/12/08/7506102/how-to-choose-a-college-that-s-right-for-you.

3. Peter Van Buskirk, "Finding a Good College Fit," *U.S. News and World Report*, June 13, 2011.

4. Bret Stephens, "Free Speech and the Necessity of Discomfort," *New York Times*, February 22, 2018.

5. Michael S. Roth, "From Unruly Hearts to Open Minds," *Inside Higher Ed*, July 17, 2017.

6. Anya Kamenetz, "What If Students Could Fire Their Professors?" *NPR Ed*, April 26, 2015.

7. David D. Perlmutter, "Academic Job Hunts from Hell: Why You Weren't Picked," *Chronicle of Higher Education*, May 30, 2016.

8. Susan J. Stabile, "The Use of Personality Tests as a Hiring Tool: Is the Benefit Worth the Cost?" *University of Pennsylvania Journal of Business Law* 4, no. 2 (2002): 279; William H. Whyte, *The Organization Man* (New York: Simon & Schuster, 1956), 182; cited in Stabile, 297n93.

9. Institute of Psychometric Coaching, "Free Practice Personality Tests," https://www.psychometricinstitute.com.au/Free-Personality-Test.asp.

10. LearnVest, "Interview Test Prep: 6 Common Personality Assessments—and How Employers Use Them," *Forbes*, May 28, 2015.

11. Frank L. Schmidt, In-Sue Oh, and Jonathan L. Shaffer, "The Validity and Utility of Selection Methods in Personnel Psychology: Practical and Theoretical Implications of 100 Years of Research Findings," working paper, *ResearchGate*, October 2016, DOI: 10.13140/RG.2.2.18843.26400.

12. See, for instance, R. E. Wildeman, G. Hofstede, Niels Noorderhaven, and A. R. Thurik, "Culture's Role in Entrepreneurship: Self-Employment out of Dissatisfaction" (Rotterdam: Rotterdam for Business Studies, 1998), https://pure. uvt.nl/portal/files/249440/annelies76587.pdf; Alexa Clay and Kyra Maya Phillips, *The Misfit Economy: Lessons in Creativity from Pirates, Hackers, Gangsters, and Other Informal Entrepreneurs* (New York: Simon & Schuster, 2015).

13. José Rolando Matalon, "When Stars Sing in the Morning," in David Birnbaum and Martin S. Cohen, *Modeh Ani*, with essays by Rachel Barenblat, Reuven P. Bulka, Martin S. Cohen et al. (New York: New Paradigm Matrix, 2017), 211–25; quotation from 223.

## AFTERWORD

1. Tomas Venclova, "At night, sleep was equivalent to time," in *Winter Dialogue: Poems*, trans. Diana Senechal (Evanston, IL: Northwestern University Press, 1997), 12.

2. Annie Polish, "Holeistic Admissions," *Contrariwise: A Journal of Philosophy* 4 (2017): 22–23.

3. Sandra Li, "Mr. Square and the Tyrannical 'Well-Rounded,'" *Contrariwise: A Journal of Philosophy* 4 (2017): 110–12.

# SELECT BIBLIOGRAPHY AND RECOMMENDED READING

## WORKS ON LANGUAGE, WORDS, AND SPEECH

Bachelard, Gaston. *On Poetic Imagination and Reverie*. Translated by Colette Gaudin. Dallas: Spring Publications, 1987.

Barthes, Roland, and Richard Havas. "Listening." In Barthes, *The Responsibility of Forms: Critical Essays on Music, Art, and Representation*. Translated by Richard Howard. New York: Hill and Wang, 1984.

Bromwich, David. *Politics by Other Means: Higher Education and Group Thinking*. New Haven, CT: Yale University Press, 1992.

Chesterton, G. K. "The Fallacy of Success." In *All Things Considered*, 21–29. New York: J. Lane, 1913.

Cockburn, Alexander, and the readers of *Counterpunch*. *Guillotined: Being a Summary Broadside Against the Corruption of the English Language*. Petrolia, CA: Counterpunch, 2012.

Cresswell, Julia. *Oxford Dictionary of Word Origins*, 2nd ed. Oxford: Oxford University Press, 2010.

Green, Jonathon. *Newspeak: A Dictionary of Jargon*. New York: Routledge, 2014.

Grice, Herbert P. *Studies in the Way of Words*. Cambridge, MA: Harvard University Press, 1989.

Harper, Douglas. *Online Etymology Dictionary*. http://www.etymonline.com/ .

Hollander, John. *The Work of Poetry*. New York: Columbia University Press, 1997.

Jacobson, Joshua. *Chanting the Hebrew Bible: The Complete Guide to the Art of Cantillation*. Philadelphia: Jewish Publication Society, 2002.

Johnson, Samuel. *A Dictionary of the English Language*. London: William Strahan, 1755.

Klein, Ernest. *A Comprehensive Etymological Dictionary of the English Language*. Amsterdam: Elsevier, 1971.

Mill, John Stuart. *On Liberty*. Edited by David Bromwich and George Kateb. New Haven, CT: Yale University Press, 2003.

Orwell, George. "Politics and the English Language." In *A Collection of Essays*. New York: Harcourt, 1981.

Pollack, John. *The Pun Also Rises: How the Humble Pun Revolutionized Language, Changed History, and Made Wordplay More Than Some Antics*. New York: Penguin, 2011.

Ravitch, Diane. *EdSpeak: A Glossary of Education Terms, Phrases, Buzzwords, and Jargon*. Alexandria, VA: Association for Supervision and Curriculum Development, 2007.

Roiphe, Katie. "The Other Whisper Network: How Twitter Feminism Is Bad for Women." *Harper's Magazine*, February 6, 2018.

Stephens, Bret. "Free Speech and the Necessity of Discomfort." *New York Times*, February 22, 2018.

Strunk, William, Jr., and E. B. White. *The Elements of Style*, 3rd ed. New York: MacMillan, 1979.

Watson, Don. *Death Sentences: How Clichés, Weasel Words, and Management Speak Are Strangling Public Language*. New York: Gotham, 2005.

White, E. B. "Freedom." In *One Man's Meat*, 205–12. New York: Harper & Brothers, 1942. Originally published under White's column "One Man's Meat" in *Harper's Magazine*, June–November 1940.

Whyte, David. *Consolations: The Solace, Nourishment, and Underlying Meaning of Everyday Words*. Langley, WA: Many Rivers Press, 2015.

Williams, Raymond. *Keywords: A Vocabulary of Culture and Society*. New York: Oxford University Press, 2015.

Woolf, Virginia. "The Decay of Essay Writing." In *Selected Essays*, 3–5. Edited by David Bradshaw. Oxford: Oxford University Press, 2009.

# WORKS ON EDUCATION, CULTURE, AND THOUGHT

Arendt, Hannah. *The Human Condition*, 2nd ed. Chicago: University of Chicago Press, 1998.

Brown, Edward James. *Mayakovsky: A Poet in the Revolution*. Princeton, NJ: Princeton University Press, 1973.

Cunningham, John. *The Miracle on South Street: The Story of Morristown's Community Theatre*. Morristown, NJ: South Street Theatre Co., 2000.

Deresiewicz, William. *Excellent Sheep: The Miseducation of the American Elite and the Way to a Meaningful Life*. New York: Free Press, 2014.

Duckworth, Angela. *Grit: The Power of Passion and Perseverance*. New York: Scribner, 2016.

Dweck, Carol. *Mindset: The New Psychology of Success*, updated ed. New York: Ballantine, 2016.

Ericsson, K. Anders, Ralf Th. Krampe, and Clemens Tesch-Römer. "The Role of Deliberate Practice in the Acquisition of Expert Performance." *Psychological Review* 100, no. 3 (1993): 363–406.

Gelman, Andrew, and Kaiser Fung. "The Power of the 'Power Pose.'" *Slate*, January 19, 2016.

Gladwell, Malcolm. *Outliers: The Story of Success*. New York: Little, Brown, 2008.

Hackman, J. Richard. "Why Teams Don't Work." (Interview with Diane Coutu.) *Harvard Business Review*, May 2009.

Heller, Nathan. "Listen and Learn." *New Yorker*, July 9, 2012.

Johnson-Laird, Philip. *How We Reason*. New York: Oxford University Press, 2008.

Li, Sandra. "Mr. Square and the Tyrannical 'Well-Rounded.'" *Contrariwise: A Journal of Philosophy* 4 (2017): 110–12.

Orr, David. *The Road Not Taken: Finding America in the Poem Everyone Loves and Almost Everyone Gets Wrong*. New York: Penguin, 2015.

Pareene, Alex. "Don't Mention Income Inequality Please, We're Entrepreneurs." *Salon*, May 21, 2012.

Petroski, Henry. *Invention by Design: How Engineers Get from Thought to Thing*. Cambridge, MA: Harvard University Press, 1996.

Polish, Annie. "Holeistic Admissions." *Contrariwise: A Journal of Philosophy* 4 (2017): 22–23.

Robinson, Ken. *Out of Our Minds: The Power of Being Creative*, 3rd ed. Chichester, UK: Capstone, 2017.

Senechal, Diana. "The Folly of the Big Idea: How a Liberal Arts Education Puts Fads in Perspective." *American Educator*, Winter 2012–2013, 15–21, 40.

————. *Republic of Noise: The Loss of Solitude in Schools and Culture.* Lanham, MD: Rowman & Littlefield, 2012.

————. "You Are Embarked: How a Philosophy Curriculum Took Shape and Took Off." *American Educator*, Spring 2015, 18–23.

Singal, Jesse. "Is Mindset Theory Really in Trouble?" The Cut, *New York Magazine*, January 18, 2017.

————. "Psychology's Favorite Tool for Measuring Racism Isn't Up to the Job." The Cut, *New York Magazine*, January 11, 2017.

Sturdy, Andrew, and Christopher Grey. "Beneath and Beyond Organizational Change Management: Exploring Alternatives." *Organization* 10, no. 4 (2003): 651–62.

Whyte, William H. *The Organization Man.* New York: Simon & Schuster, 1956.


# LITERARY AND PHILOSOPHICAL WORKS

Aristotle. *Nicomachean Ethics.* Translated by Robert C. Bartlett and Susan D. Collins. Chicago: University of Chicago Press, 2011.

Bromwich, David. *Moral Imagination: Essays.* Princeton, NJ: Princeton University Press, 2014.

Buber, Martin. *I and Thou.* Translated by Ronald Gregor Smith. New York: Scribner, 2000.

*Contrariwise: A Journal of Philosophy*, by students of Columbia Secondary School for Math, Science, and Engineering. New York: Columbia Secondary School, 2014–.

Dante Alighieri. *The Divine Comedy.* Translated by Allen Mandelbaum. New York: Everyman's Library, 1995.

Frost, Robert. *The Poetry of Robert Frost: The Collected Poems, Complete and Unabridged.* Edited by Edward Connery Lathem. New York: Henry Holt, 1979.

King, Martin Luther, Jr. *A Testament of Hope: The Essential Writings and Speeches of Martin Luther King, Jr.* Edited by James M. Washington. New York: HarperCollins, 1991.

Krasznahorkai, László. *The Last Wolf; and Herman: "The Game Warden," "The Death of a Craft."* Translated by George Szirtes and John Batki. New York: New Directions, 2016.

Mayakovsky, Vladimir. "Oblako v shtanakh: tetraptikh." In *Stikhotvoreniia, poemy.* Moscow: Khudozhestvennaia literatura, 1986.

Melville, Herman. *Moby-Dick.* New York: Norton, 2002.

O'Connor, Flannery. *Wise Blood.* New York: Noonday, 1967.

Plato. *Republic.* Translated by G. M. A. Grube. Revised by C. D. C. Reeve. Indianapolis: Hackett, 1992.

Plutarch. "On Listening to Lectures." In *Moralia*, vol. 1, 243–45. Translated by F. C. Babbitt. Cambridge, MA: Harvard University Press, 1927.

Rawls, John. *Political Liberalism*, expanded ed. New York: Columbia University Press, 2005.

Saunders, George. *Pastoralia: Stories.* New York: Riverhead, 2000.

Whitehead, Alfred North. *Process and Reality.* New York: Free Press, 1978.

# INDEX

# ABOUT THE AUTHOR

**Diana Senechal**, a teacher, writer, and scholar, is the 2011 winner of the Hiett Prize in the Humanities and a valued contributor to literary and cultural discussion. Her translations of the poetry of Tomas Venclova have appeared in two books: *Winter Dialogue* (1997) and *The Junction* (2008). Her first book, *Republic of Noise: The Loss of Solitude in Schools and Culture* (Rowman & Littlefield Education, 2012) was named an Outstanding Academic Title of 2012 by Choice; the poet Rosanna Warren praised its "erudition and quiet wisdom." Senechal has given interviews and talks around the United States; published nonfiction, poetry, and fiction in blogs and magazines; and spoken on BBC World Service's flagship program, *The Forum*.

A Yale University graduate (BA, MA, and PhD), she began public school teaching in 2005. From 2011 to 2016, she taught philosophy at Columbia Secondary School for Math, Science, and Engineering, where she created a high school philosophy curriculum, taught courses and mentored teachers, and guided her students in the creation and publication of the philosophy journal *Contrariwise*, which now has international readership and participation. In May 2017, she taught as a guest lecturer at the Lycée Sainte Pulchérie in Istanbul; she now teaches English and civilization at the Varga Katalin Gimnázium in Szolnok, Hungary.

She serves on the council of the Association of Literary Scholars, Critics, and Writers and on the faculty of the Dallas Institute of Humanities and Culture's Sue Rose Summer Institute for Teachers. At her Budapest synagogue, Szim Salom, she serves in a cantorial role. In her free time, she does volunteer work for the Budapest Festival Orchestra, memorizes poetry in various languages, and goes exploring on bicycle.